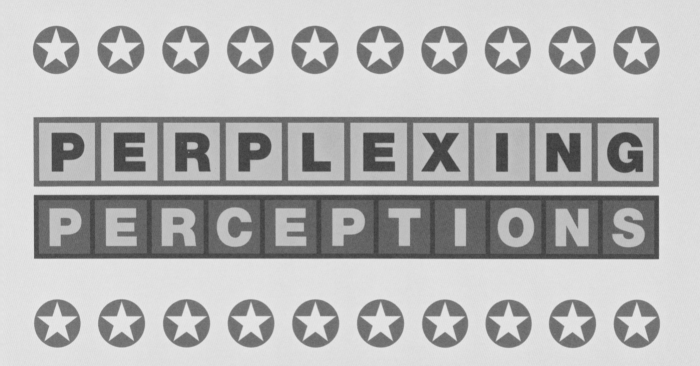

PERPLEXING PERCEPTIONS

THUNDER BAY
P·R·E·S·S
San Diego, California

Thunder Bay Press

An imprint of the Advantage Publishers Group

5880 Oberlin Drive, San Diego, CA 92121-4794

www.thunderbaybooks.com

Published by arrangement with Book Creation Ltd., London, and Book Creation, LLC, New York.

All notations of errors or omissions should be addressed to Thunder Bay Press, Editorial Department, at the above address. All other correspondence (author inquiries, permissions) concerning the content of this book should be addressed to Book Creation Ltd., 20 Lochaline Street, London W6 9SH, United Kingdom; E-mail: info@librios.com

ISBN 1-59223-353-8

Printed and bound in China

1 2 3 4 5   09 08 07 06 05

I n this volume of *Perplexing Perceptions* we'll be improving your skills in two and three dimensions and hopefully having fun along the way.

The ability to perceive things in three dimensions is becoming more important in our everyday lives. Computer programs are now able to take a two-dimensional image, such as a photograph, and apply it to a three-dimensional model so that a full-perspective image of a human face can be rendered. This technology can be used to help catch criminals or to see your face on the main character in a computer game! Inventors are currently looking at methods to produce 3-D television, and even more basic 3-D style images such as holograms now play an important part in security and forgery protection.

The main theory of perception is called "perceptual constancy." This means that, even though we see a car close to us in the street, we would know how that object would behave if we saw it again in the distance or on television. This also explains why our senses can become easily confused. When we go into a hall of mirrors at the fair or look at an optical illusion, our previous experience works against us and provides confusing yet amusing results. It is also the basis of some visual comedy and fun vacation photo snaps, when objects can appear out of scale.

Perceptions also have their place in art. Bridget Riley (1931–) is a leading figure in op art, the artistic movement where flat paintings give the impression of a 3-D surface. And, of course, there are the classic engravings and woodcuts of the Dutch graphic artist M. C. Escher (1898–1972), with his impossible-looking staircases.

Is there such a thing as ESP (extrasensory perception)? The debate between scientists and believers has raged for many decades. In 1853, the famous physicist Michael Faraday tried an experiment that involved a group of people trying to tilt a table. His conclusion was that the sitters were moving the table, not paranormal forces. In 1995, the CIA released some of its findings from over twenty years of research and claimed that, although such abilities had been demonstrated in their laboratories, the skills had little practical use. Sometimes a radio is much simpler to use than a mind reader!

So, before you dive headlong into the book, here's a few words of advice. All the puzzles have a time limit as a guide, but if you'd prefer to proceed at your own pace . . . who's to know?! You can just open the book and find a puzzle that looks interesting. However, as that doesn't narrow it down much, be sure to pay attention to our special star grading system. Easier puzzles have one, two, or three stars. Eight, nine, or (ouch) ten stars means you're in danger of going boggle-eyed. You have been warned.

Our perception is that you're going to get a lot of enjoyment out of the puzzles within, so we won't delay you a moment more. Have fun. ✪

—David Bodycombe

1 **DIFFICULTY** ✪✪✪✪✪✪✪✪✪✪  **3** **Minutes**

Travel from one star's center to the other's center without crossing any lines.

2 DIFFICULTY ✪✪✪✪✪✪✪✪✪✪   5 Minutes

Using only straight lines, can you divide this rectangle into eight sections, each of identical shape and size, and each with four red circles?

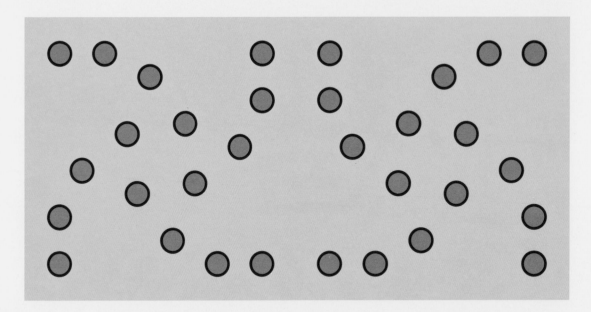

3 DIFFICULTY ✪✪✪✪✪✪✪✪✪✪   2 Minutes

Here are four matches. Can you move one match to leave two?

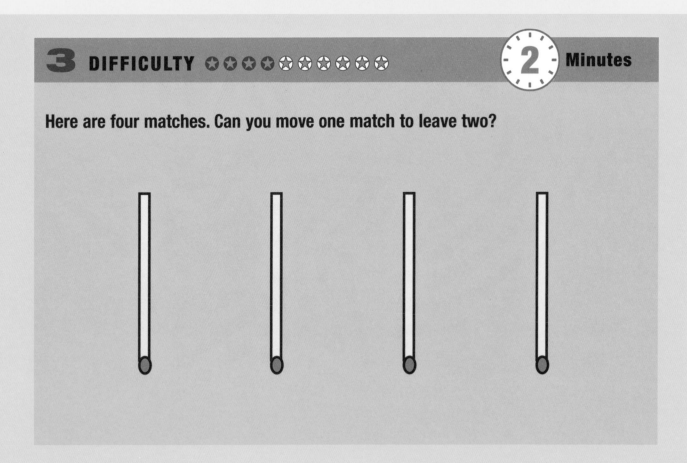

4 **DIFFICULTY** ✪✪✪✪✪✪✪✪✪✪  **4** **Minutes**

Can you pair this stamp with its correct print?

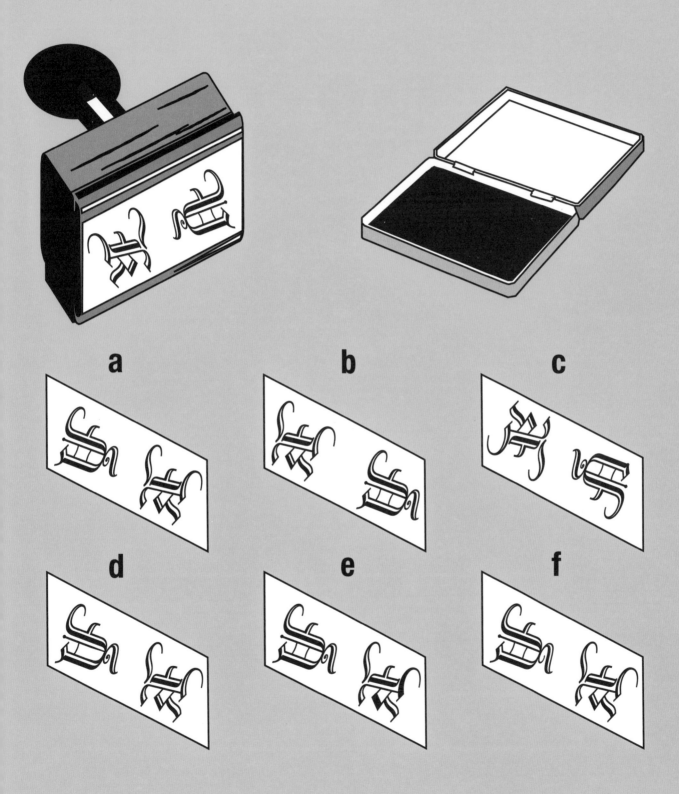

a

b

c

d

e

f

5 DIFFICULTY  **3** Minutes

Which of the four boxed figures (a, b, c, or d) completes the set?

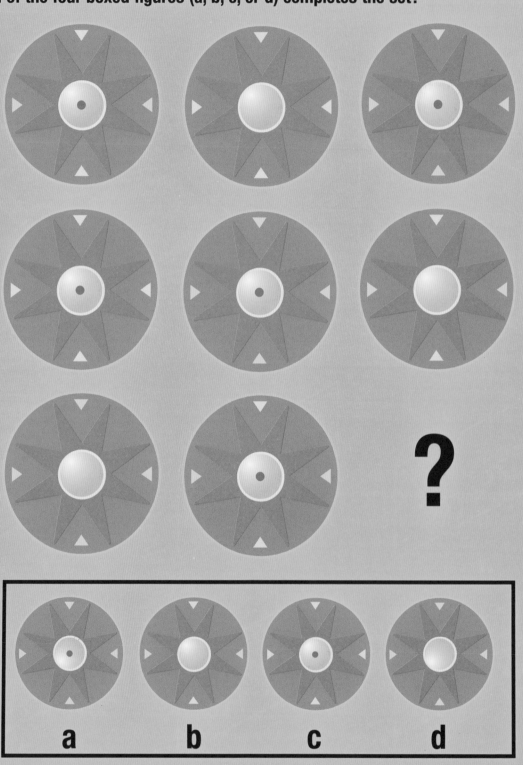

6 DIFFICULTY ✪✪✪✪✪✪☆☆☆☆

6 Minutes

A famous mathematical theorem says that any political map (where no two bordering countries are colored the same) can be completed using just four colors. Grab four different pens and see if you can color the mainland of Europe correctly. Don't worry about the small islands.

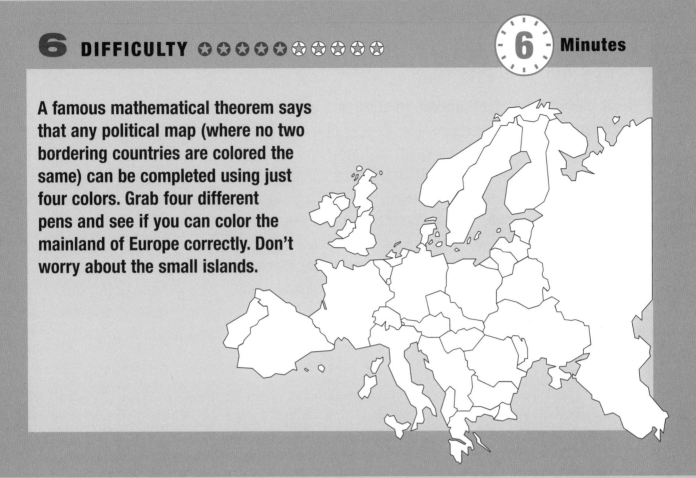

7 DIFFICULTY ✪✪✪☆☆☆☆☆☆☆

3 Minutes

Can you cut this cake into four slices, each containing the same number and type of decorations, with just two straight cuts of the knife? Although the knife may pass between the candles, no decoration may be cut!

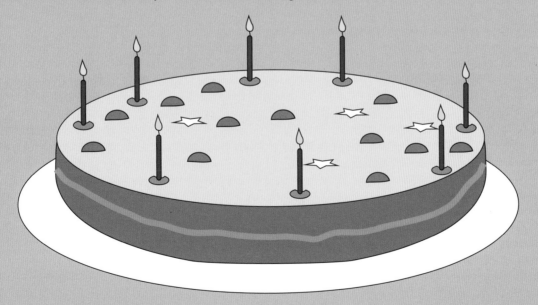

8 DIFFICULTY ✪✪✪✪✪☆☆☆☆☆  **8** **Minutes**

Kirsty played a game of Snakes and Ladders with her brother Tom. He threw the first 6, so started first, placing his playing piece on the 6. After that, every time it was Kirsty's turn, her die followed the sequence 6, 4, 2, 5, 3, 1; so her first move was to square 6, her second was to square 10, her third was to 12, etc. After his first turn when he threw the 6, Tom's die followed the sequence 2, 4, 6, 1, 3, 5 each time, so his second move was to square 8, his third was to 12, etc. The normal rules of the game were followed, so whenever someone landed on a square that had the foot of a ladder, the piece was moved to the top of the ladder. Whenever someone landed on a square that had the head of a snake, the piece was moved to the tail of the snake. The number thrown to end the game didn't necessarily matter, since the first person to move a piece completely off the board won. Who won the game—Kirsty or Tom?

100	99	98	97	96	95	94	93	92	91
81	82	83	84	85	86	87	88	89	90
80	79	78	77	76	75	74	73	72	71
61	62	63	64	65	66	67	68	69	70
60	59	58	57	56	55	54	53	52	51
41	42	43	44	45	46	47	48	49	50
40	39	38	37	36	35	34	33	32	31
21	22	23	24	25	26	27	28	29	30
20	19	18	17	16	15	14	13	12	11
1	2	3	4	5	6	7	8	9	10

START →

9 DIFFICULTY ⭐⭐⭐⭐✩✩✩✩✩✩ **2** Minutes

Keith's magic mirror reflects very strangely! Can you match each leaf to its correct (although misplaced and somewhat distorted) image in the mirror?

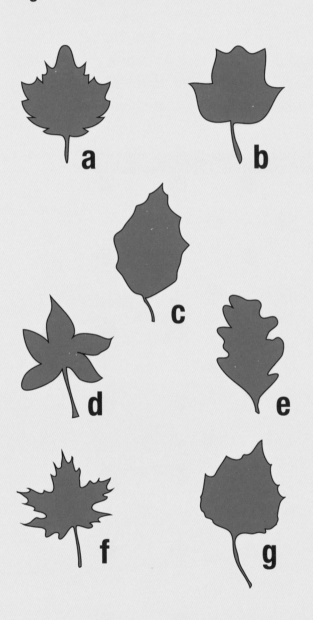

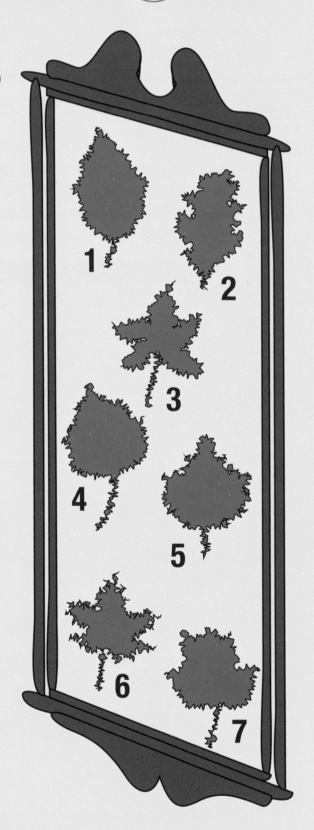

10 DIFFICULTY ✪✪✪✪✪✪☆☆☆☆

In this two-player game, the aim is to make a continuous path in your color across the board. Choose a red or blue pen, then decide who goes first. To begin, the first player draws a line from any dot of his or her color to the nearest dot horizontally or vertically next to it. The second player does the same between two dots of their own color.

Players continue to make moves in turns. Because each player is using his or her own set of dots and paths, there cannot be a tie. Lines must not cross at any point. The winner is the first player to achieve a continuous path in his or her color, from his or her starting side to the opposite edge.

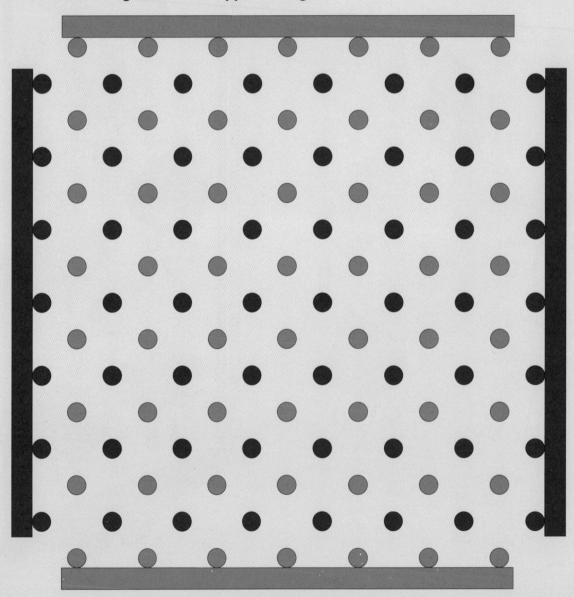

11 DIFFICULTY ✪✪✪✪✪✪✪✪✪✪

8 Minutes

In each of the four buildings below, one type of brick is used more or less frequently than it is in the other three buildings. Can you discover the different brick in each construction? The ten brick types are as follows:

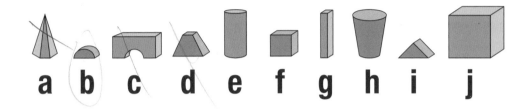

a b c d e f g h i j

Building 1

Building 2

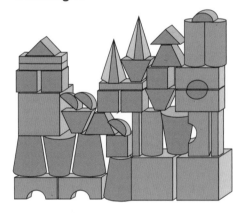

Building 3

Building 4

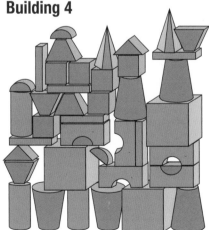

12 DIFFICULTY ✪✪✪✪✪✪✪✪✪✪   ③ Minutes

At the local casino, they play a dice gambling game that involves throwing two dice and betting a stake of $12. What are the rules and how much did Gary Gambler win or lose when he threw a 2 followed by a 3? Study the clues below to discover the answer.

1. Gina threw a 4 followed by a 5 and got $6 back, losing $6.

2. Gordon threw a 1 followed by a 5 and broke even, so got $12 back.

3. Graham threw a 1 followed by a 3 and got $24 back, so won $12.

13 DIFFICULTY ✪✪✪✪✪✪✪✪✪✪   ④ Minutes

By drawing three straight lines, can you divide this room into five sections, each containing a bed, a storage unit, a table, and two chairs?

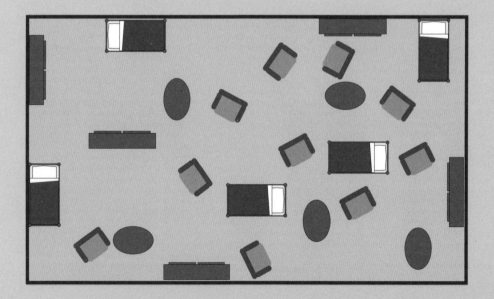

14 DIFFICULTY ✪✪✪✪✪✪✪☆☆☆  **Minutes**

A circular loop of string lies flat on a table. Part of the string has been hidden from view by the black border. If X is inside the loop, what can you say about Y? Here's a hint: coloring in some of the areas may help you.

15 DIFFICULTY ✪✪✪✪✪✪☆☆☆☆  **Minutes**

Which three pieces can be fitted together to form an identical copy of this shape? Pieces may be rotated, but not flipped over.

a b c d

e f g h i

j k l m

n o p q

16 DIFFICULTY ✪✪✪✪✪✪☆☆☆  **4** **Minutes**

Try to make your way to the center of this circular maze.

17 DIFFICULTY ✪✪✪✪✪✪✪✪✪✪

5 Minutes

Can you spot the eight differences between these two pictures? Circle them in the lower drawing.

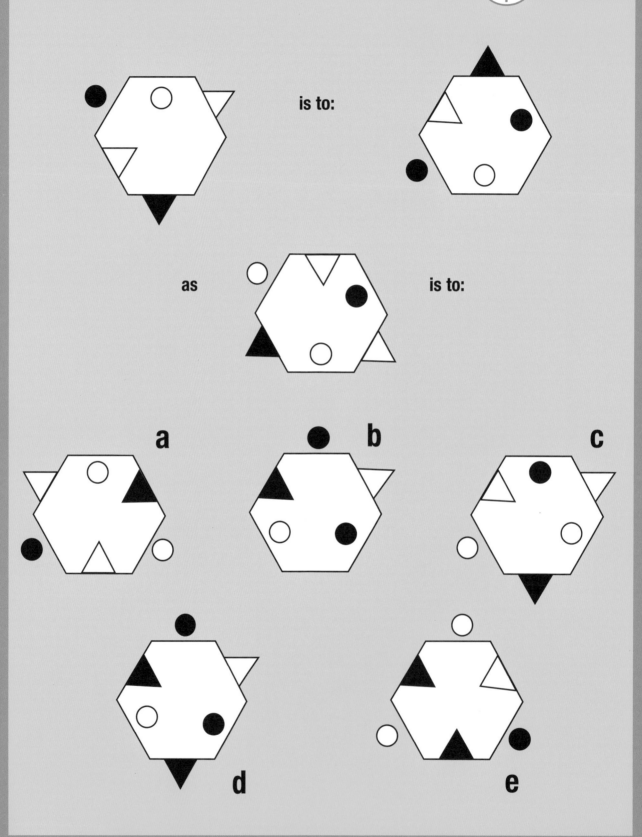

is to:

as

is to:

a

b

c

d

e

19 DIFFICULTY ✪✪✪✪✪✪✪✩✩✩  4 Minutes

When the shape below is folded into a cube, which one of the following
(a, b, c, d, or e) is produced?

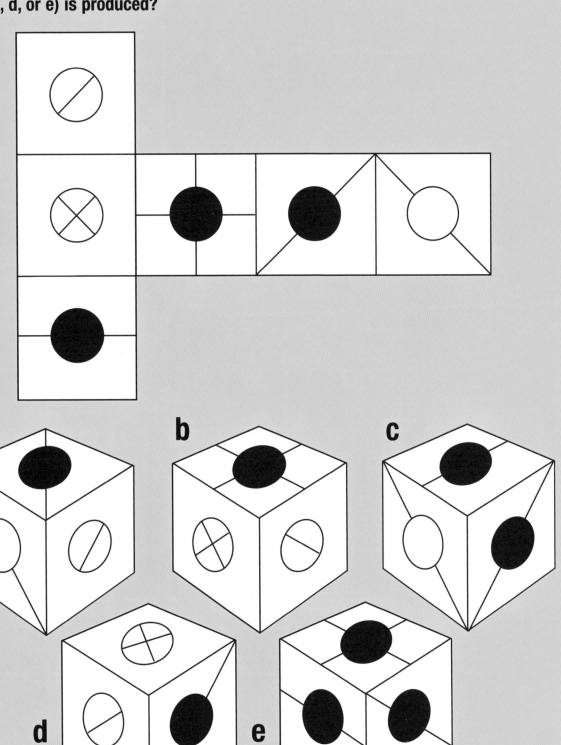

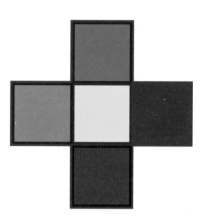

This cross is hidden only once in the large grid of squares below. The pattern may be rotated but not reflected. Can you find it?

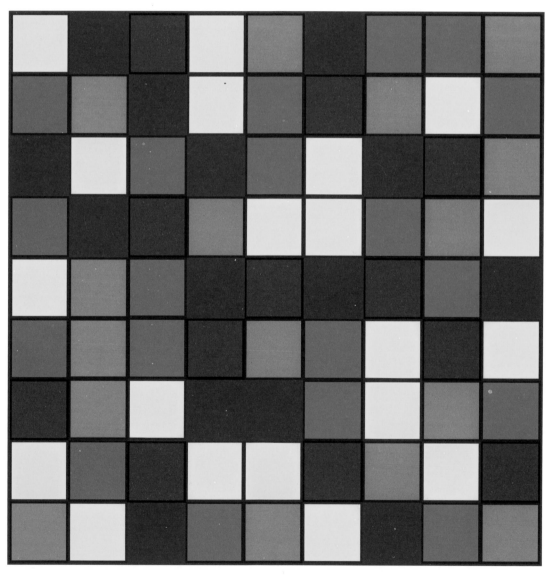

21 DIFFICULTY ✪✪✪✪✪✪✪✩✩✩

30 Minutes

Think deeply and you might find a way to complete this numeropic.

How to do a numeropic:

Along each row or column, there are numbers that indicate how many blocks of black squares are in a line. For example, "3, 4, 5" indicates that from left to right or top to bottom, there is a group of three black squares, then a group of four black squares, then another group of five black squares.

Each block of black squares on the same line must have at least one white square between it and the next block of black squares. Blocks of black squares may or may not have a number of white squares before and after them.

It is sometimes possible to determine which squares will be black without reference to other lines or columns. It is helpful to put a small dot in a square you know will be empty.

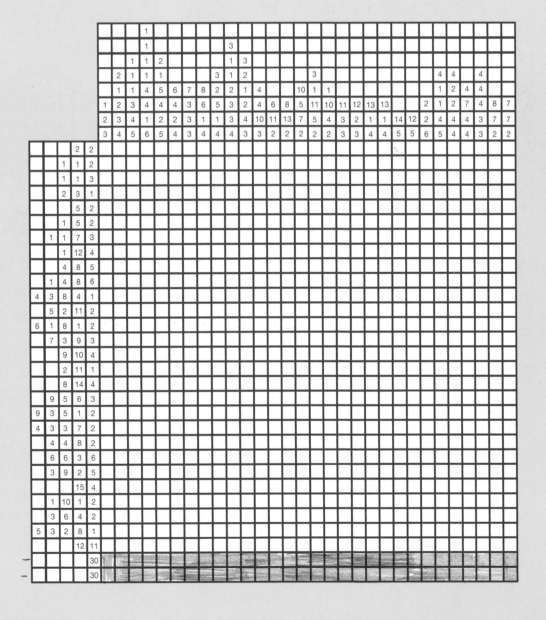

30 X 30

22 DIFFICULTY ✪✪✪✪✪✪✪✪✪✪  **5** Minutes

What shape should be in the middle?

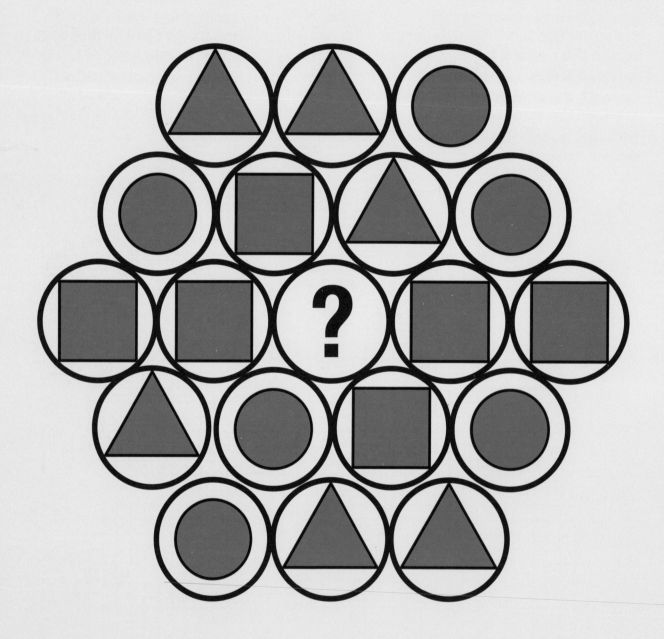

23 DIFFICULTY ✪✪✪✪✪✪✪☆☆

6 Minutes

How many differences can you spot between these two pictures, given that one is supposed to be an exact mirror image of the other? Circle them in the drawing on the right.

24 DIFFICULTY ✪✪✪✪✪☆☆☆☆

5 Minutes

Using three of the four different mathematical operators (+, −, x, ÷), can you find the correct totals for each of these dice problems?

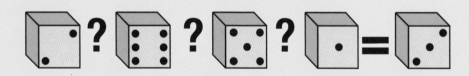

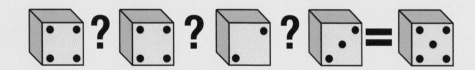

25 DIFFICULTY ✪✪✪✪✪✩✩✩✩✩    **5** Minutes

When the shape below is folded into a cube, which one of the following (a, b, c, d, or e) is produced?

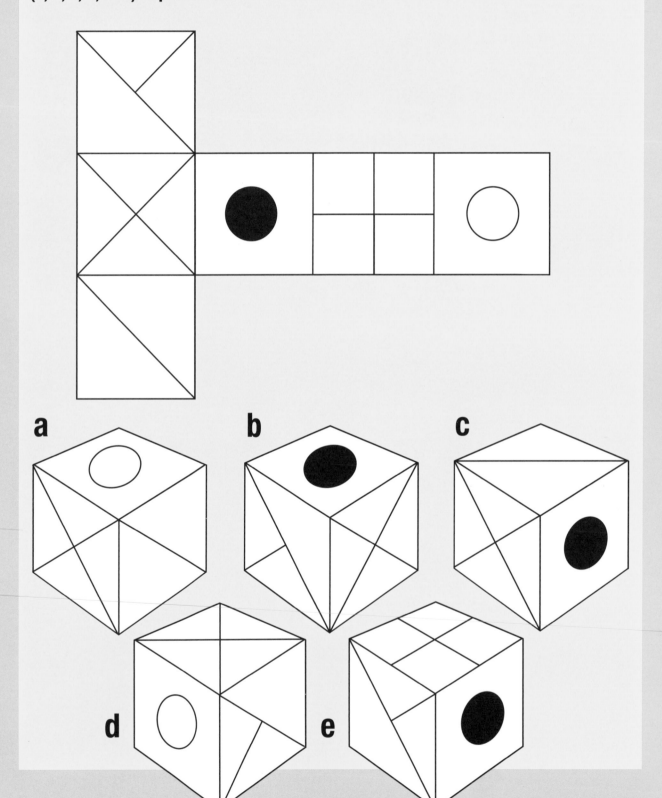

26 DIFFICULTY ✪✪✪✪✪✪✪✪✪✪ ⏱ 1 Minute

Study this picture for one minute, then see if you can answer the questions on page 28.

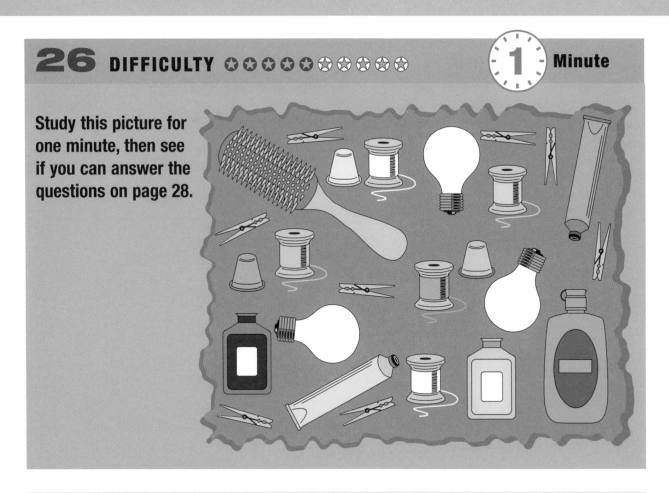

27 DIFFICULTY ✪✪✪✪✪✪✪✪✪✪ ⏱ 2 Minutes

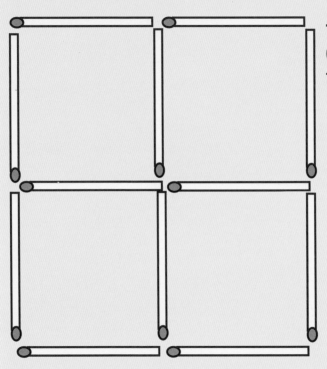

These matches make five squares. Can you move two to make five triangles?

[26] DIFFICULTY ✪✪✪✪✪☆☆☆☆☆  3 Minutes

Can you answer these questions about the puzzle on page 27 without looking back?

1. What color is the hairbrush?

2. How many thimbles appear in the picture?

3. What color is the tube at the top right corner of the picture?

4. How many lightbulbs appear in the picture?

5. How many spools of thread have white thread?

6. How many clothespins appear in the picture?

7. How many bottles have a white label?

8. How many objects are in the picture?

28 DIFFICULTY ✪✪✪✪☆☆☆☆☆☆ 3 Minutes

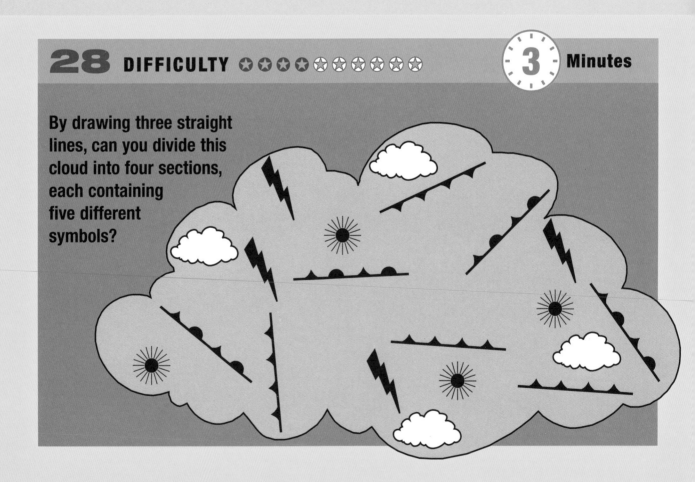

By drawing three straight lines, can you divide this cloud into four sections, each containing five different symbols?

29 DIFFICULTY ✪✪✪✪✪✪✪✪✪✪  **4** **Minutes**

Starting at a, see if you can make your way to b in this difficult triangular maze.

What is the missing shape?

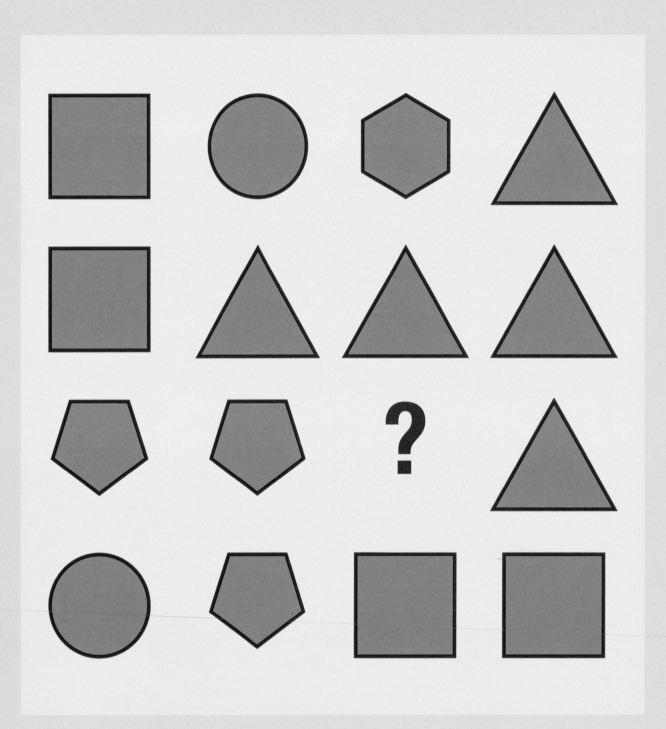

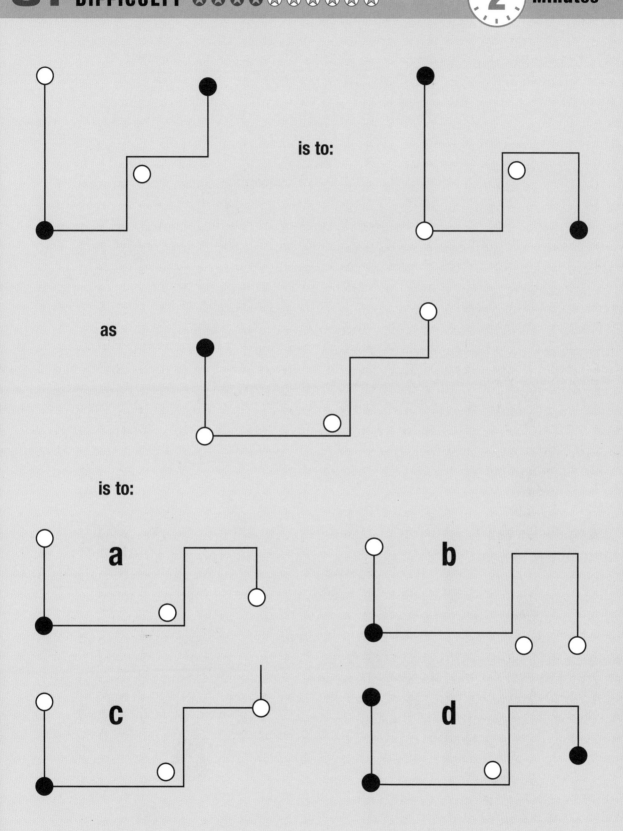

32 DIFFICULTY ⭐✩✩✩✩✩✩✩✩✩

4 Minutes

These ducks are identical except for one.
Which one is different from the rest?

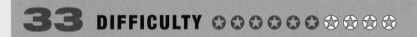

33 DIFFICULTY ⭐✩✩⭐✩✩⭐✩✩✩

4 Minutes

Which pieces can
fit together to form
an identical copy
of this clock?

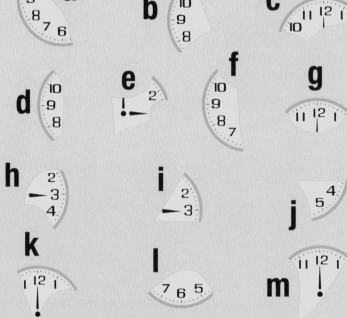

34 DIFFICULTY ✪✪✪✪✪✪✪✪✪✪ ⟨2⟩ Minutes

Study this picture for two minutes, then see if you can answer the questions on page 34.

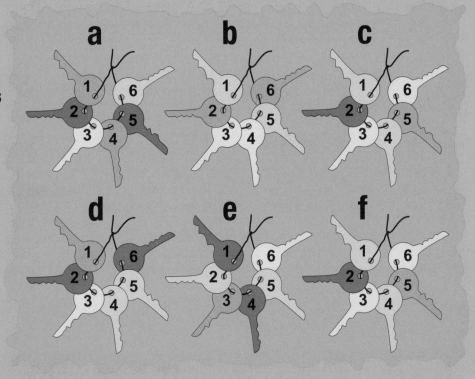

35 DIFFICULTY ✪✪✪✪✪✪✪✪✪✪ ⟨4⟩ Minutes

By drawing three straight lines, can you divide this rectangle into four sections, each containing eight different birds?

[34] DIFFICULTY ✪✪✪✪✪✪✪✪✪✪  **3** Minutes

Can you answer these questions about the puzzle on page 33 without looking back?

1. How many keys are there in total?

2. Which two bunches of keys are identical?

3. How many blue keys appear in total?

4. Which letter identifies the key ring with no red keys?

5. How many keys with the number 6 are yellow?

6. Which letter identifies the key ring with two blue keys touching one another?

7. How many odd-numbered keys are purple?

8. Which letter identifies the only key ring with a purple key numbered 6?

36 DIFFICULTY ✪✪✪✪✪✪✪✪✪✪ **4** Minutes

Here are ten matches. What is the smallest number you have to take away to leave two?

37 DIFFICULTY ✪✪✪✪✪✪✪✪✪✪ ② Minutes

Which number should follow in this dice sequence?

23   **14**   **8**   **?**

38 DIFFICULTY ✪✪✪✪✪✪✪✪✪✪ ⑤ Minutes

Juliette has lined up these three dice on her coffee table. She can see the same seven faces that you can see. Angelica (her friend, sitting opposite) can see the top three faces of the dice, as well as another four faces you and Juliette cannot see. None of you can see the bottom three faces of these dice. What is the total number of spots on all the faces of the dice that Angelica can see, given that this is a different number from the total number of dots you can see?

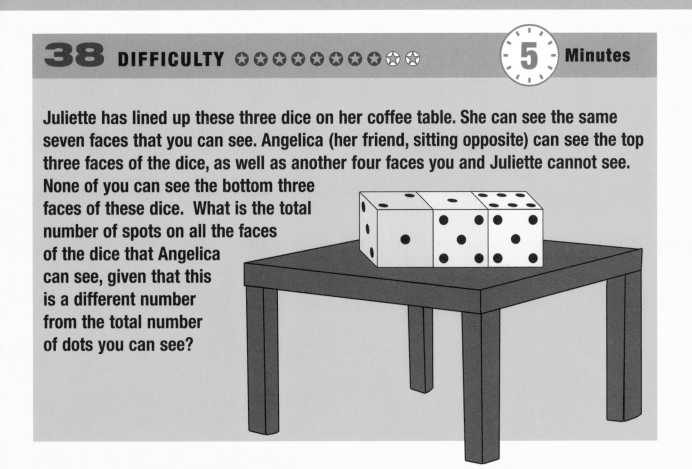

39 DIFFICULTY ✪✪✪✪✪✪☆☆☆☆  **30** Minutes

Face facts in order to complete this numeropic. Refer to the instructions on page 23 for help on how to do this kind of puzzle.

Column clues (top):

								1										2								
						1	1	2										2	5	5	3					
						2	2	1										2	2	2	2					
				1	1	1	1	1	1	1								2	2	2	2					
		1		2	2	1	1	1	2	2				2	2		2	2	2	2	1					
	1	2	1	14	14	7	4	2	9	9	1	1	1	1	1	2	2	2	2	2	2	5	5	3	1	
	7	14	2	1	1	1	1	1	1	1	1	2	2	2	2	8	8	8	2	2	2	2	5	5	3	1
3	5	7	3	5	23	5	5	5	11	13	13	13	25	25	25	25	1	9	9	2	2	2	2	5	5	3	1

Row clues (left):

			15
		13	6
		13	7
			4
		13	7
	4	6	6
			13
	4	6	6
	6	6	7
	6	11	4
7	1	9	7
		19	6
			20
	9	7	6
		20	7
	5	7	4
		16	7
		13	6
	1	8	2
	12	2	6
1	8	2	7
1	8	2	4
	13	2	7
	13	2	6
		14	2
		14	2
		14	2
			7
			8

40 DIFFICULTY ✪✪✪✪✪✪✪✪✪✪ **4** Minutes

David's magic mirror reflects very strangely! Can you match each lamp to its correct (although misplaced and somewhat distorted) image in the mirror?

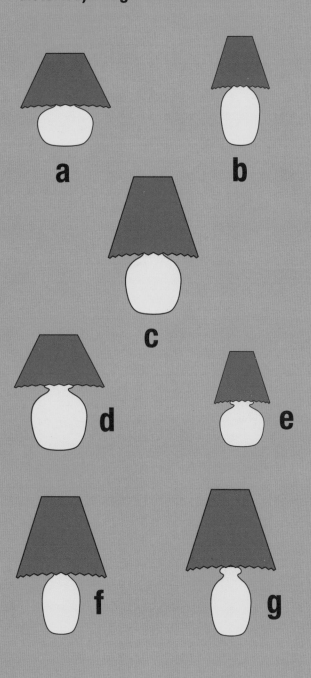

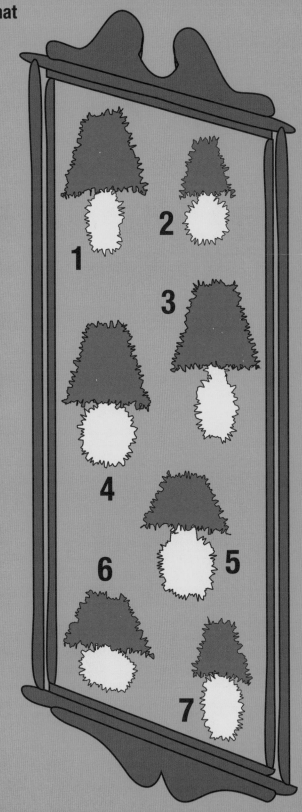

41 DIFFICULTY ✪✪✪✪✪✪✪✪✪✪  **4** Minutes

Carefully study the rocking horses below. Which is different from the rest?

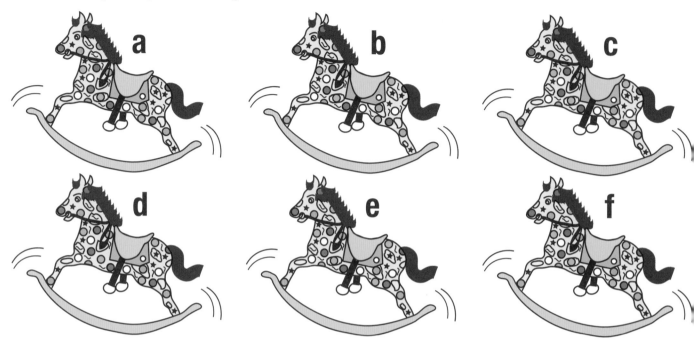

42 DIFFICULTY ✪✪✪✪✪✪✪✪✪✪  **3** Minutes

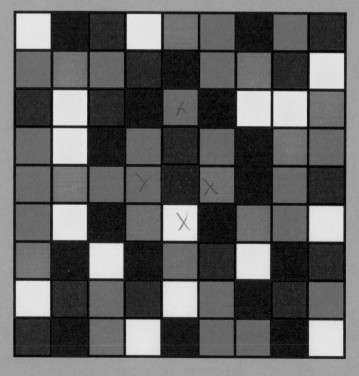

Where can the cross be found in the larger grid? The pattern may be rotated but not reflected.

43 DIFFICULTY ✪✪✪✪☆☆☆☆☆☆

4 Minutes

Using three colored pens (e.g., red, yellow, and blue), color in this diagram so that no two bordering areas have the same color.

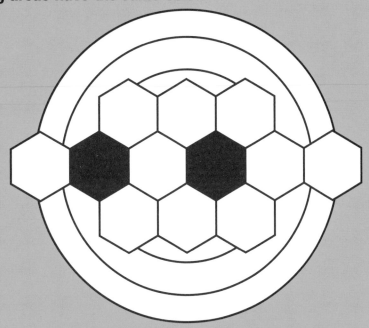

44 DIFFICULTY ✪✪✪✪✪☆☆☆☆☆

5 Minutes

Using straight lines only, can you divide this T-shirt into sections, each containing the same number of differently colored T-shirts?

45 DIFFICULTY ✪✪✪✪✪✪✪✪✩✩✩  **8** Minutes

Starting at the top hexagon in the maze, make your way to the bottom hexagon by moving from shape to adjacent shape. You may ONLY move from a blue shape to a green one, from a green shape to a red one, or from a red shape to a blue one.

46 DIFFICULTY ✪✪✪✪✪✪✩✩✩✩  Minutes

Can you spot the ten differences between these two pictures?
Circle them in the lower drawing.

47 DIFFICULTY ✪✪✪✪✪✪✪✪✪✪ ⏱ **6** Minutes

Mary would like to buy two identical T-shirts for her twin brothers. Which two should she buy?

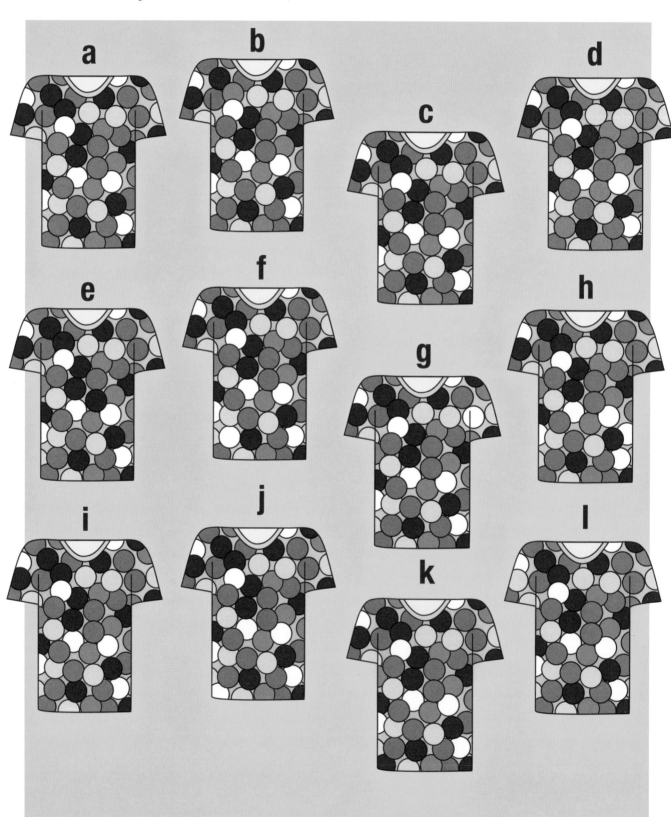

48 DIFFICULTY ✪✪✪✪✪✪✩✩✩✩  Minutes

In each of the four buildings below, one type of brick is used more or less frequently than it is in the other three buildings. Can you discover the different brick in each construction? The ten brick types are as follows:

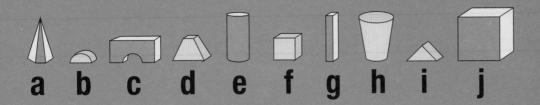

a b c d e f g h i j

Building 1

Building 2

Building 3

Building 4

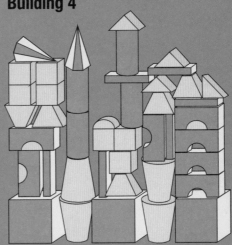

49 **DIFFICULTY** ✪✪✪✪✪✪✪✪✪  **4** **Minutes**

What shape is missing?

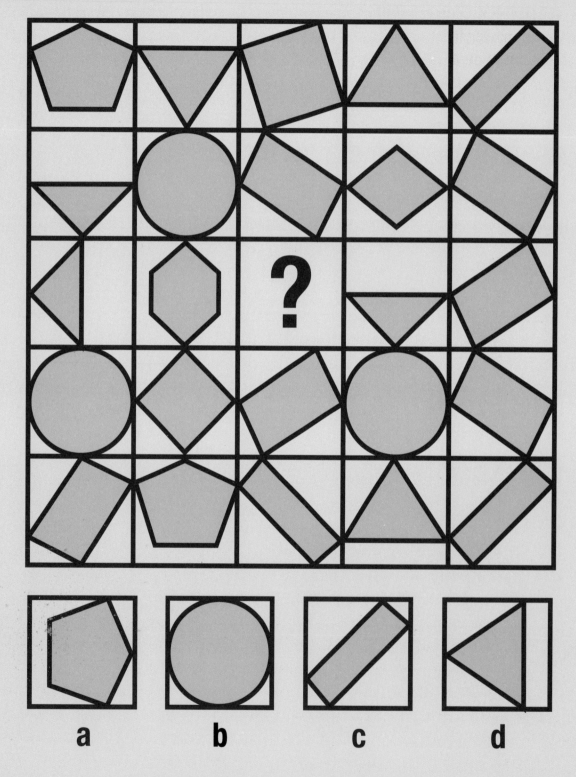

50 DIFFICULTY ✪✪✪✪✪✪☆☆☆☆  **Minutes**

Study this picture for two minutes, then see if you can answer the questions on page 46.

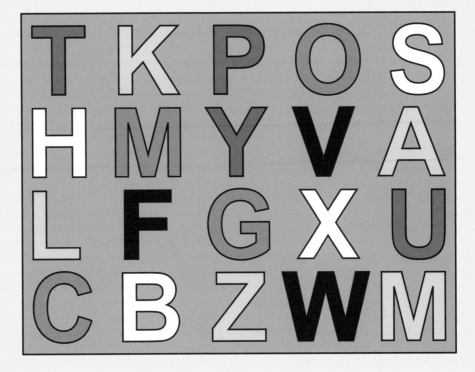

51 DIFFICULTY ✪✪✪✪✪✪✪☆☆☆  **Minutes**

Think laterally to make a perfect square out of these four heptagonal coins.

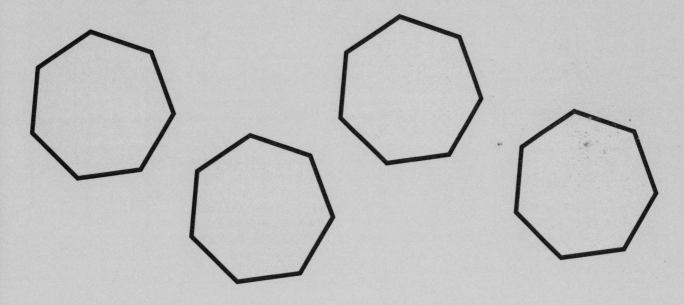

[50] DIFFICULTY ✪✪✪✪✪✪✪✪✪✪ **3** Minutes

Can you answer these questions about the puzzle on page 45 without looking back?

1. Which letter appears twice?

2. Which color is used for more letters than any other color?

3. What color is the Y?

4. What color is the letter above the Y?

5. Which letter is directly below the F?

6. Which letter is between the C and the H?

7. What color is the V?

8. Which letter is left of the S?

52 DIFFICULTY ✪✪✪✪✪✪✪✪✪✪ **4** Minutes

It is not possible to color in this diagram with just three different pens so that no two bordering areas have the same coloring. Can you manage it by resorting to a fourth color for only one area?

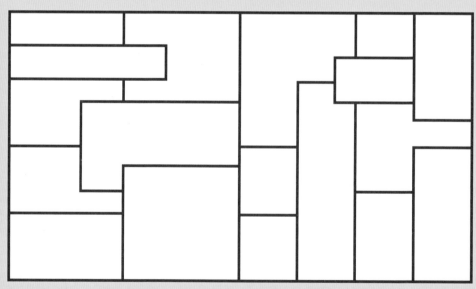

53 DIFFICULTY ✪✪✪✪✪✪✪✪✪✪

In this two-player network game, all you need to start are three + signs drawn on a piece of paper. The first player connects up any two of the "crossroads" and adds a third + sign somewhere along that route, in effect adding two new spur roads. The second player does the same, making sure that the lines do not cross. The play continues back and forth between both players until no valid move can be made.

The illustration shows the first three moves in a sample game.

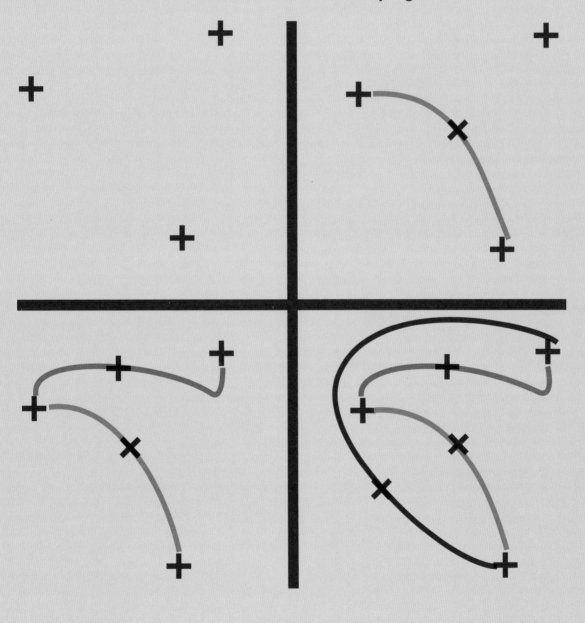

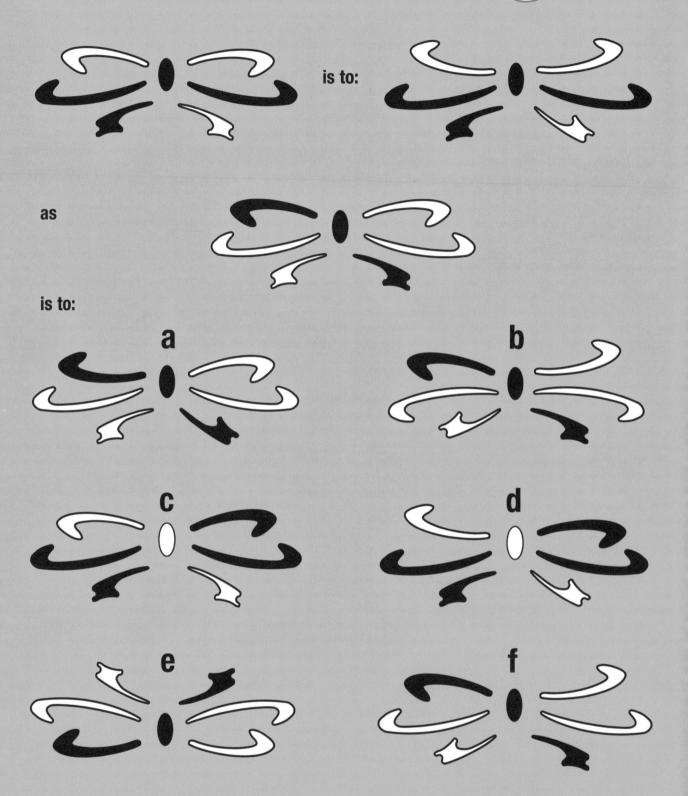

55 DIFFICULTY ✩✩✩✩✩✩✩✩✩✩

30 Minutes

Make the connections between the numbers to complete this numeropic.
See page 23 for instructions on how to complete this kind of puzzle.

Column clues (top):

									3	3																			
							3	3	1	1	3	3																	
				4	4	5	4	4	2	2	5	5	2	2	4	4	5	4	4										
	6	6		7	4	5	4	5	5	6	5	2	2	5	6	5	5	4	5	4	7								
6	6	12	12	7	6	2	6	10	12	12	6	5	5	5	5	6	12	12	10	6	2	6	7	6	6	6	6		
4	6	11	1	1	17	9	7	5	4	3	3	2	2	1	1	2	2	3	3	4	5	7	9	17	15	15	11	6	4
6	2	2	2	2	2	2	2	2	2	2	2	2	2	2	2	2	2	2	2	2	2	2	2	2	2	2	2	2	6

Row clues (left):

			12	
			16	
			20	
		11	11	
		9	9	
	7	2	2	7
	7	2	2	7
		7	14	7
	7	6	6	7
		4	2	4
		5	6	5
		4	10	4
		5	12	5
		5	12	5
	4	6	6	4
	4	5	5	4
4	5	2	5	4
4	5	2	5	4
	5	5	5	5
	5	6	6	5
		6	12	6
		7	12	7
		8	10	8
		9	6	9
	3	7	2	12
		3	9	14
			30	
		1	1	
			30	
			30	

56 DIFFICULTY ✪✪✪✪✪✪✪☆☆  **3** Minutes

Can you match this potted plant with its shadow?

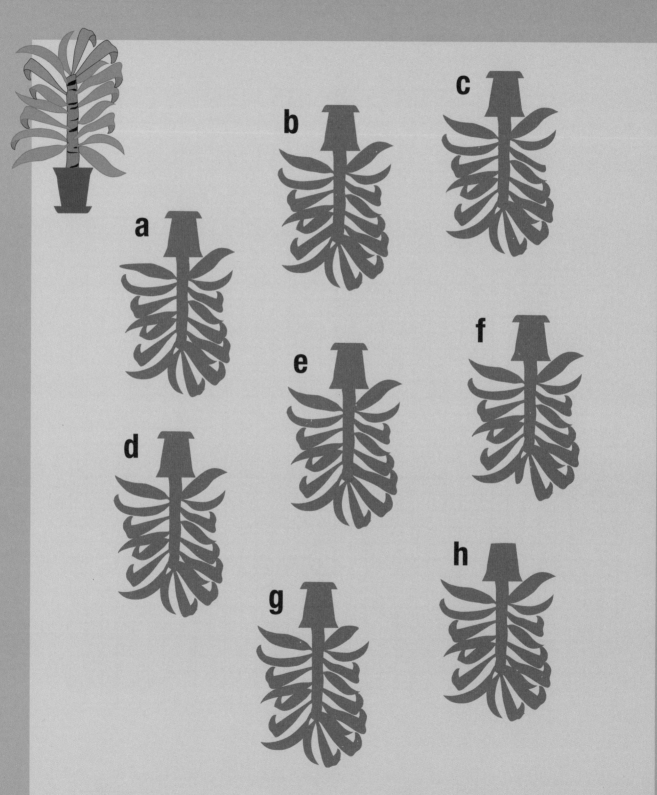

57 DIFFICULTY ✪✪✪✪✪✪✪✪☆☆

 **Minutes**

Travel from any star on the top row of the grid to any star on the bottom row by moving from one square in the grid to an adjacent one. You may ONLY move from a star to a square, from a square to a circle, or from a circle to a star. You may not move diagonally. Colors are only there to confuse.

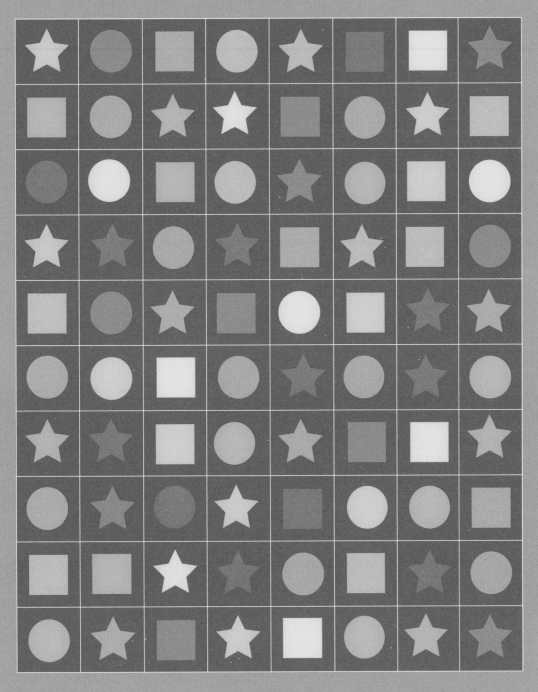

58 DIFFICULTY ✪✪✪✪✪✪☆☆☆☆   ⏱ **2** Minutes

These matches make eight triangles. Can you take away three matches to leave four?

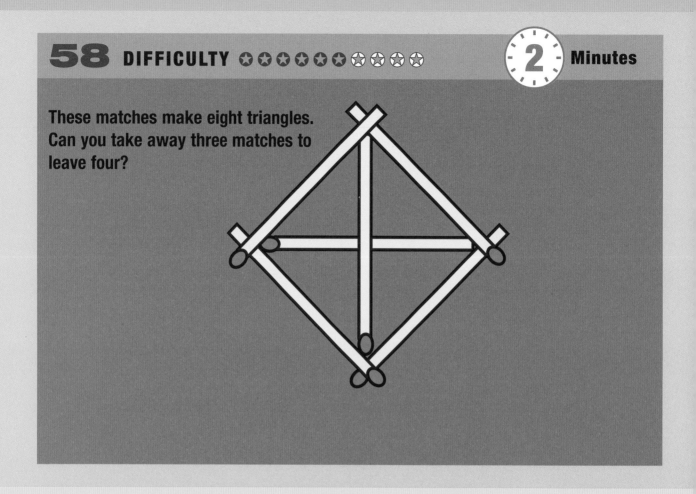

59 DIFFICULTY ✪✪✪✪✪✪✪☆☆☆   ⏱ **4** Minutes

When the shape on the right is folded into a cube, which one of the following (a, b, c, d, or e) is produced?

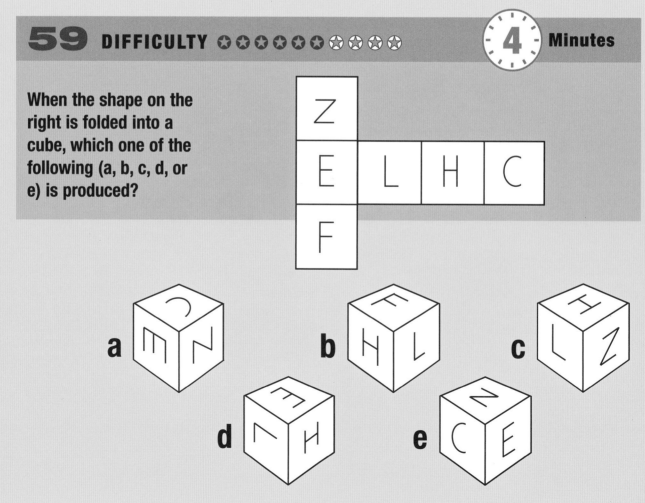

60 DIFFICULTY ✪✪✪✪✪✪☆☆☆☆ ③ Minutes

These balls have been kicked around, but all are identical except for one. Which one is different from the rest?

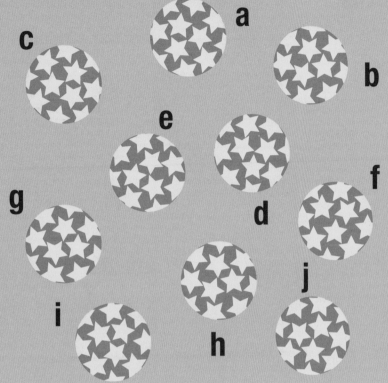

61 DIFFICULTY ✪✪☆☆☆☆☆☆☆☆ ⑤ Minutes

Can you spot the ten differences between these two pictures? Circle them in the drawing on the right.

62 DIFFICULTY ✪✪✪✪✪✪✪✪✪✪ ⏱ **3** Minutes

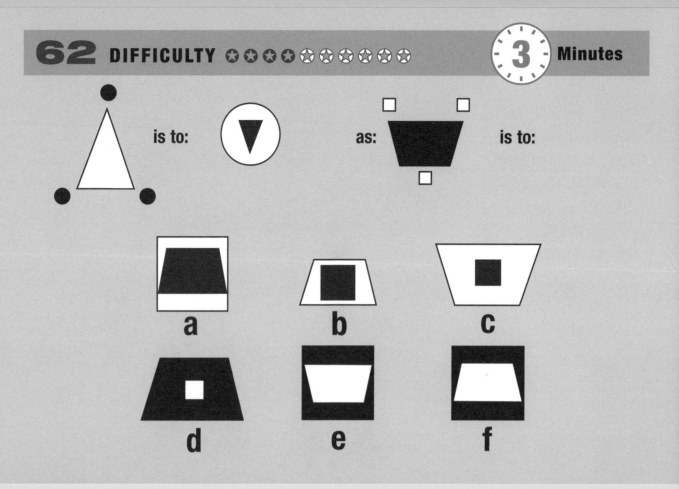

a   b   c

d   e   f

63 DIFFICULTY ✪✪✪✪✪✪✪✪✪✪ ⏱ **5** Minutes

At the local casino, they play a dice gambling game, which involves throwing two dice and betting a stake of $6. What are the rules and how much did Gary Gambler win or lose when he threw a 6 followed by a 1? Study the clues below to discover the answer.

1. Gina threw a 3 followed by a 2 and got $2 back, so lost $4.

2. George threw a 2 followed by a 6 and got $8 back, thus won $2.

3. Graham threw a 4 followed by a 1 and got $6 back, so broke even.

64 DIFFICULTY ✪✪✪✪✪✪✪✪✪✪

 **2** Minutes

Study this picture for two minutes, then see if you can answer the questions on page 56.

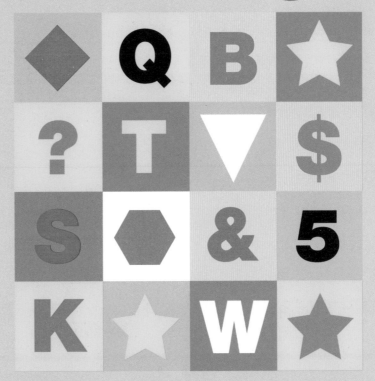

65 DIFFICULTY ✪✪✪✪✪✪✪✪✪✪

4 Minutes

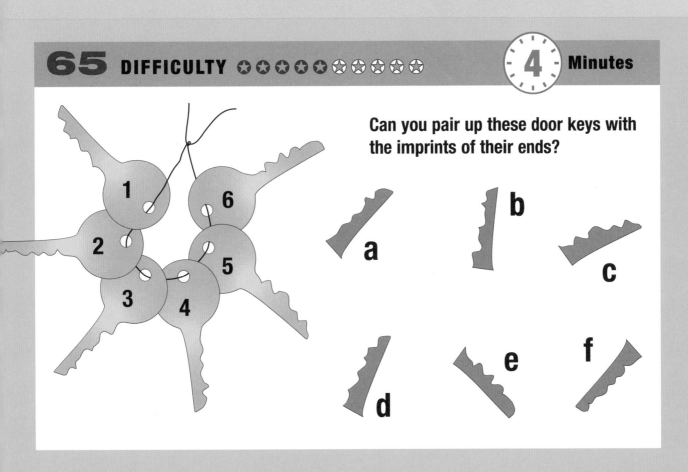

Can you pair up these door keys with the imprints of their ends?

[64] DIFFICULTY ✪✪✪✪✪✪✪✪✪✪  Minutes

Can you answer these questions about the puzzle on page 55 without looking back?

1. Which number appears on a square with a blue background?

2. What is the color of the letter K?

3. What color is the question mark?

4. What color is the triangle?

5. Which letter appears above the K?

6. How many letters appear on squares with a green background?

7. How many yellow stars appear in the picture?

8. Which letter appears diagonally between the letter S and the letter B?

66 DIFFICULTY ✪✪✪✪✪✪✪✪✪✪  Minutes

What is the sum total of the spots on the fifteen hidden sides of these four dice?

In how many different places can the shape shown be found in the larger grid? The pattern may be rotated but not reflected.

68 DIFFICULTY ★☆☆☆☆☆☆☆☆

10 Minutes

Kirsty played a game of Snakes and Ladders with her brother Tom. He threw the first 6, so started first, placing his playing piece on the 6. After that, every time it was Kirsty's turn, her die followed the sequence 6, 5, 4, 3, 2, 1; so her first move was to square 6, then square 11, etc. After his first turn when he threw the 6, Tom's die followed the sequence 1, 2, 3, 4, 5, 6 each time, so his second move was to square 7, his third was to 9, etc. The normal rules of the game were followed, so whenever someone landed on a square that had the foot of a ladder, the piece was moved to the top of the ladder. Whenever someone lands on a square that had the head of a snake, the piece was moved to the tail of the snake. The number thrown to end the game didn't necessarily matter, since the first person to move a piece completely off the board won. Who won the game—Kirsty or Tom?

100	99	98	97	96	95	94	93	92	91
81	82	83	84	85	86	87	88	89	90
80	79	78	77	76	75	74	73	72	71
61	62	63	64	65	66	67	68	69	70
60	59	58	57	56	55	54	53	52	51
41	42	43	44	45	46	47	48	49	50
40	39	38	37	36	35	34	33	32	31
21	22	23	24	25	26	27	28	29	30
20	19	18	17	16	15	14	13	12	11
1	2	3	4	5	6	7	8	9	10

START →

69 DIFFICULTY ★☆★☆☆☆☆☆☆☆  **Minutes**

Can you spot the ten differences between these two pictures? Circle them in the drawing on the right.

70 DIFFICULTY ★★★★★☆☆☆☆☆  **3** Minutes

These witches are identical except for one. Which witch is different from the rest?

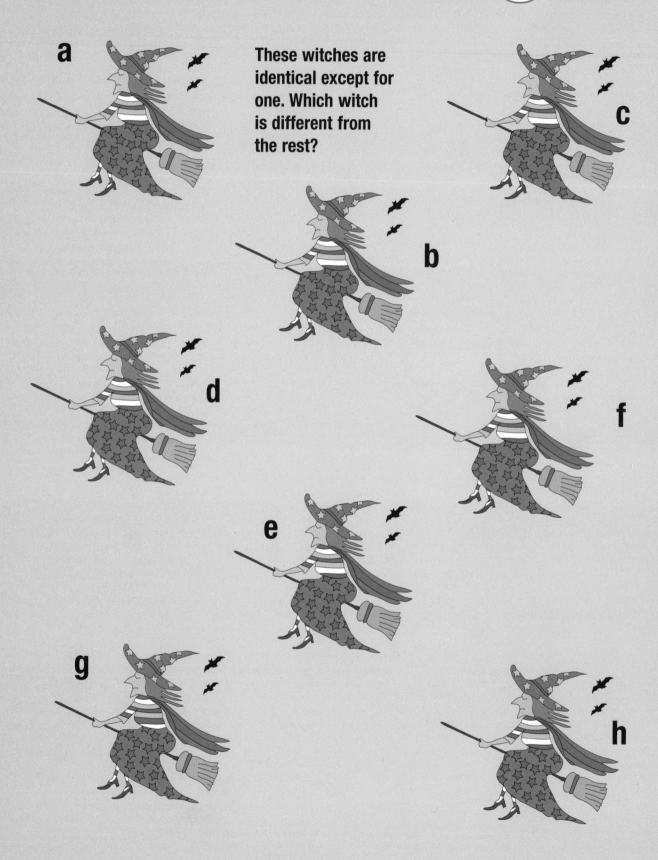

71 DIFFICULTY ✪✪✪✪✪☆☆☆☆☆  **6** Minutes

Use four different colored pens to shade in this diagram like a political map so that no two bordering areas have the same color. It's trickier than it looks!

72 DIFFICULTY ✪✪✪✪✪✪☆☆☆☆  **3** Minutes

Look carefully—which of the ten clock hands is in the wrong position? Where should it be instead?

73 DIFFICULTY ✪✪✪✪✪✪✪✪✪✪

4 Minutes

Mrs. R. Teest would like to buy two identical abstract paintings, but is rather confused by the choice at the art gallery. Can you help by finding two that are exactly the same?

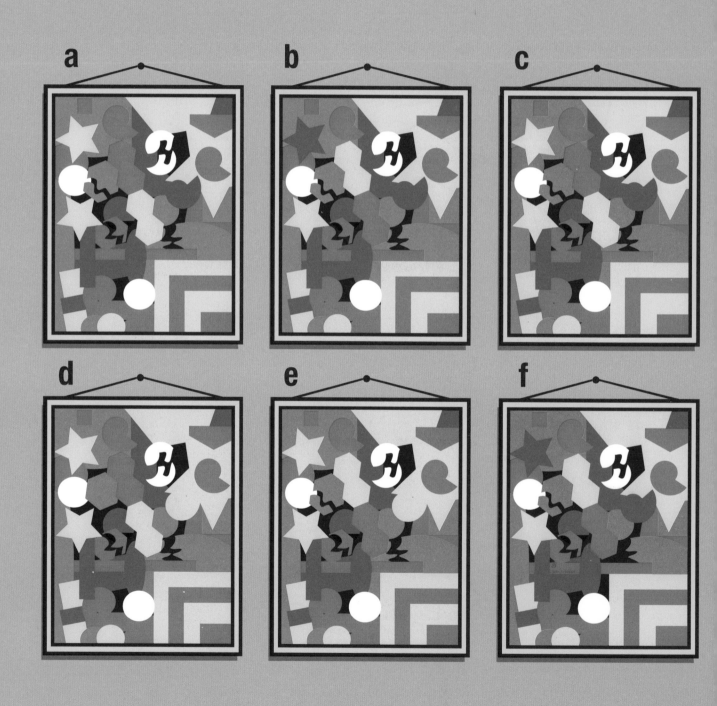

74 DIFFICULTY ✪✪✪✪✪✪✪✪✪✪

 **3** Minutes

Make your way from A to B collecting just one of each of the four shapes. You can pick them up in any order but you may NOT travel over the same path more than once.

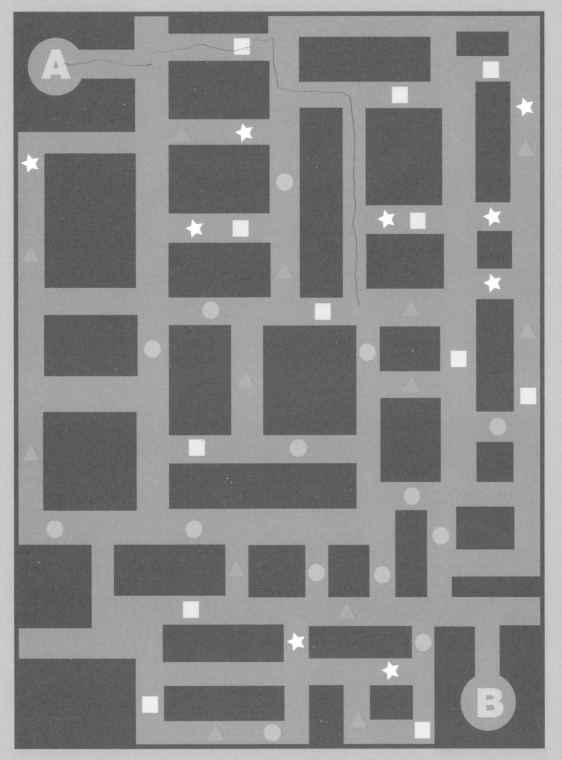

75 DIFFICULTY ✪✪✪✪✪✪✩✩✩✩  **5** **Minutes**

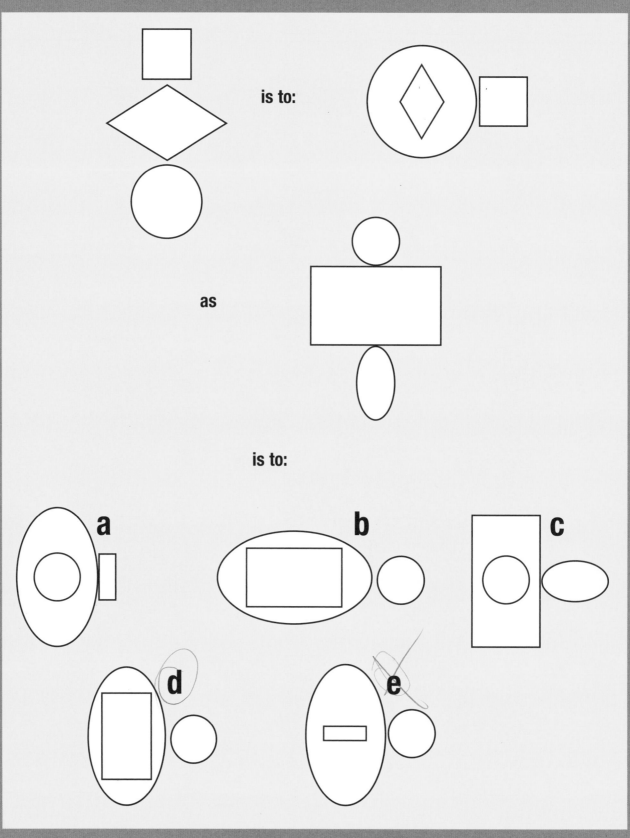

76 DIFFICULTY ✪✪✪✪✪✪✪✪✪✪ **6** Minutes

In how many different places can the pattern shown be found in the grid below? The pattern may be rotated but not reflected.

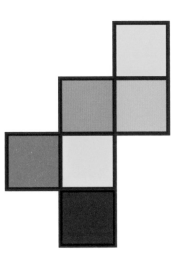

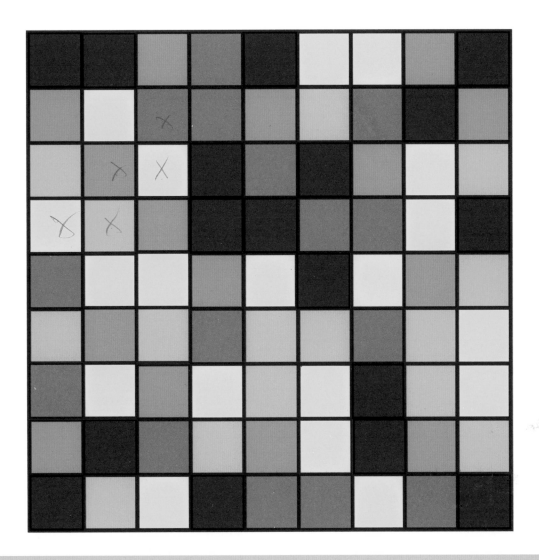

77 DIFFICULTY ☆☆☆☆☆☆☆☆☆ **30 Minutes**

Once you've completed this numeropic, you'll never forget how it's done. See page 23 for instructions on how to complete this type of puzzle.

(Numeropic / nonogram puzzle)

Left-side (row) clues, top to bottom:

- 1 2 1
- 2 2 2
- 3 2 1 1
- 3 2 1
- 4 14 2
- 18
- 5 13
- 6 13
- 7 2 13
- 7 4 12
- 3 7 12
- 4 7 12
- 8 2 13
- 8 1 14
- 4 4 1 14
- 1 2 5 1 14
- 8 15
- 10 15
- 5 5 15
- 3 19
- 3 4 4 2 4
- 2 4 4 2 4
- 2 4 4 2 4
- 2 1 2 1 2 2 1 2
- 2
- 2 1 14
- 2 15 1
- 1 7 2 3 2
- 6 2 2 6
- 30

Top (column) clues, as printed:

| | | | | 2 | | | | | | | | | | | | | | | | | | | | | | | | | | | |
| 3 |
1		2	3	3					3
3	2	2	1	8	3				3	2	2	3	4	5						1	2	3
1	1	2	11	3	1	4		5	3	8	5	8	10	12	20	16	20	20	16	20	19	1	19	16	12	10
3	2	4	17	7	1	1	7	14	19	13	7	5	2	2	2	2	2	3	3	2	2	3	3	19	2	2	1	1	2
1	1	1	1	1	1	1	1	2	3	3	3	4	4	1	1	2	2	1	1	2	2	1	1	5	2	2	3	3	2

78 DIFFICULTY ✪✪✪✪✪✪✪✪✪

 **6** Minutes

At first glance, these photos may look identical. However, only two are exactly the same. Can you spot them?

a

b

c

d

e

f

79 DIFFICULTY ✪✪✪✪✪✪✪✪✪✪

4 Minutes

Can you spot the eight differences between these two seasonal pictures? Circle them in the lower drawing.

80 DIFFICULTY ✪✪✪✪✪✪✪✪✪✪

3 Minutes

Can you rearrange these matches so that the area enclosed is twice as large?

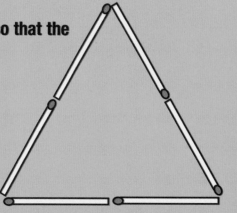

81 DIFFICULTY ✪✪✪✪✪✪✪✪✪  **4** Minutes

Which of the figures below (a, b, or c) completes the grid above?

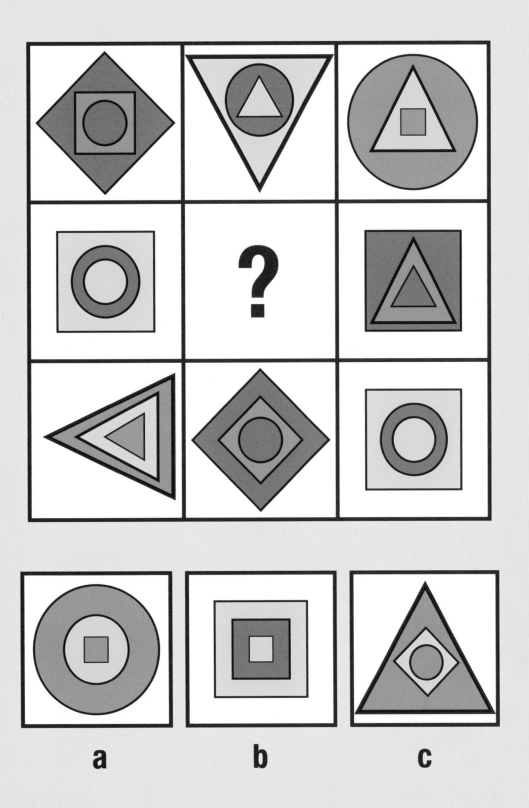

a　　　　b　　　　c

82 DIFFICULTY ✪✪✪✪✪✪✪✪✪ ⏱ **5** Minutes

Which three pieces can fit together to match the chair on the right? Any piece may be rotated, but not flipped over.

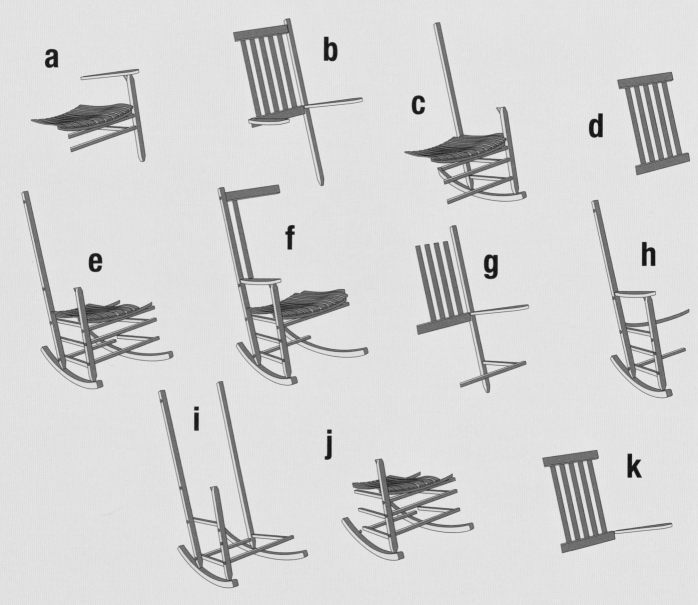

83 DIFFICULTY ✪✪✪✪✪✪☆☆☆☆  4 Minutes

Where can this specific pattern of squares be found in the larger grid? The pattern may be rotated but not reflected.

84 DIFFICULTY ✪✪✪✪✪☆☆☆☆☆ 4 Minutes

Arrange these fourteen coins into seven lines of four coins each.

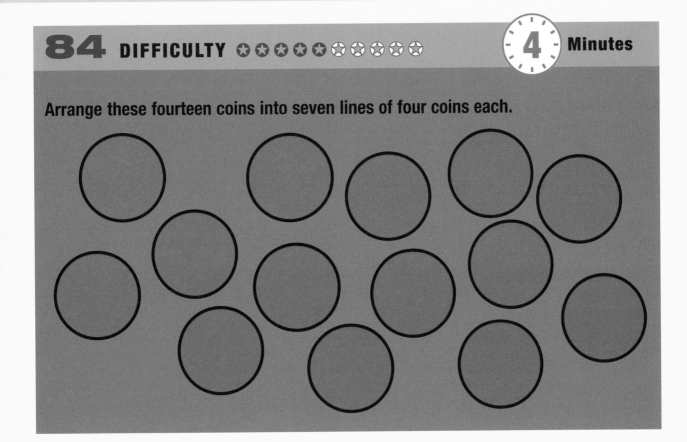

85 DIFFICULTY ✪✪✪✪✪✪☆☆☆☆

3 Minutes

By drawing four straight lines, can you divide this shape into five sections, each containing seven letters?

A Y M T S F S T X F A A Y T F T X M Y M S Y T X S F Y A M X M S X F A X S

86 DIFFICULTY ✪✪✪✪✪☆☆☆☆☆

3 Minutes

All of these aliens are odd, but which is the odd one out?

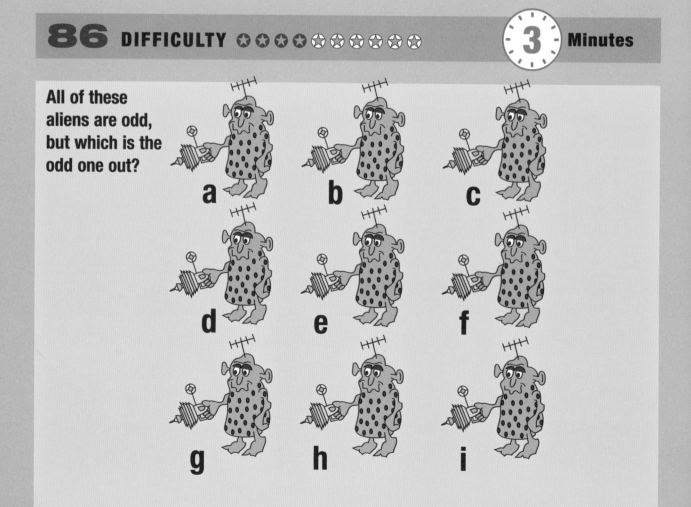

a   b   c

d   e   f

g   h   i

87 DIFFICULTY ✪✪✪✪✪✪✩✩✩✩ 2 Minutes

Study this picture for two minutes, then see if you can answer the questions on page 74.

88 DIFFICULTY ✪✪✪✪✪✪✩✩✩✩ 3 Minutes

Which number should follow next in this dice sequence?

36   **12**   **4**   **?**

[87] DIFFICULTY ✪✪✪✪✪✪✪✪✪✪  **3** Minutes

Can you answer these questions about the puzzle on page 73 without looking back?

1. How many white-petaled flowers have white centers?

2. How many blue-petaled flowers appear in total?

3. How many blue-petaled flowers have blue centers?

4. What color petals does the flower at the very tip of the leaf have?

5. How many red-petaled flowers have yellow centers?

6. How many white-petaled flowers appear in total?

7. What is the total number of flowers in the picture?

8. How many petals does each flower have?

89 DIFFICULTY ✪✪✪✪✪✪✪✪✪✪  **6** Minutes

In how many different places can the pattern shown be found in the larger grid? The pattern may be rotated but not reflected.

90 DIFFICULTY ✪✪✪✪✪✪✪✪✪✪ 4 Minutes

Can you draw appropriate-colored lines from dot to dot (e.g., a yellow line from yellow dot to yellow dot) so that all the pairs of dots are connected up? None of the colored lines may cross or touch, even at a corner.

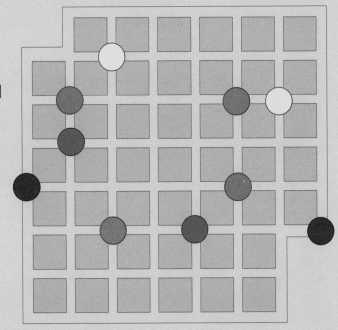

91 DIFFICULTY ✪✪✪✪✪✪✪✪✪✪ 4 Minutes

When this shape is folded to form a cube, which is the only one of the following that can be produced?

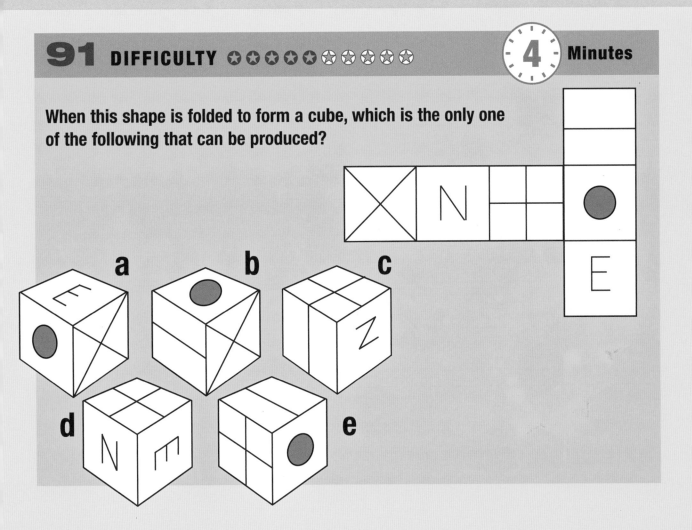

92 **DIFFICULTY** ✪✪✪✪✪✪✪✪✪✪ **7** Minutes

Can you match the picture of gardening tools and a wheelbarrow with its silhouette?

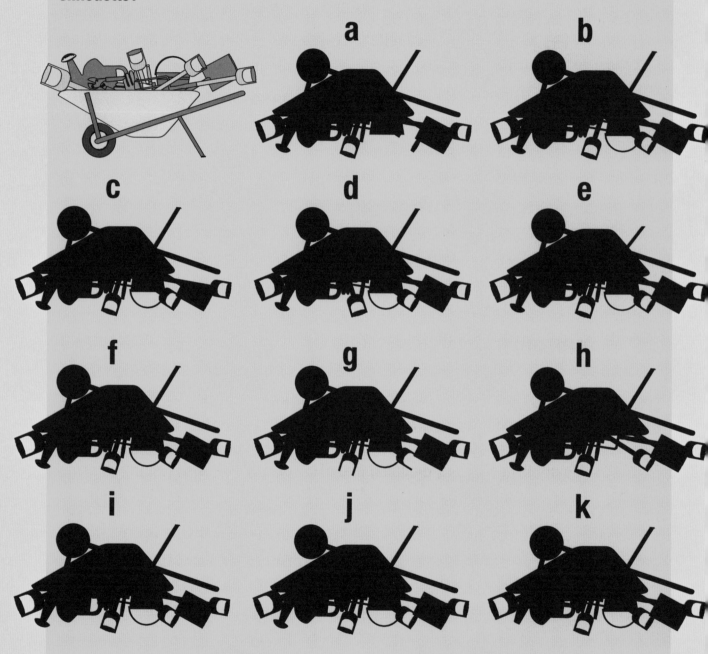

93 DIFFICULTY ✪✪✪✪✪✪✪✪✪✪ ② Minutes

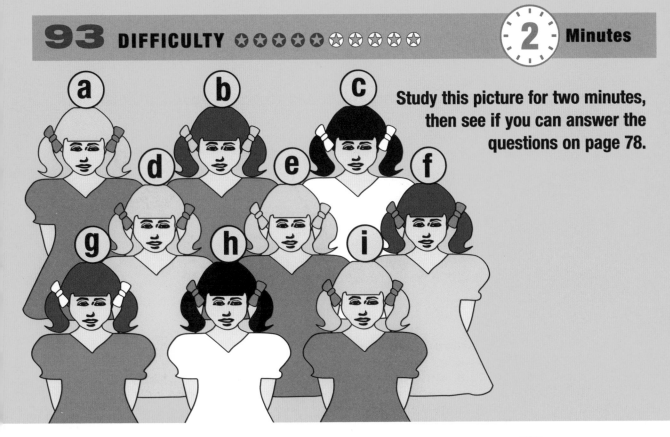

Study this picture for two minutes, then see if you can answer the questions on page 78.

94 DIFFICULTY ✪✪✪✪✪✪✪✪✪✪ ⑧ Minutes

The square below contains exactly one of each of 36 faces from six standard dice. In each horizontal row of six smaller squares and each vertical column of six smaller squares, there are faces with different numbers of spots. There is no die face with five spots in the long diagonal line of six smaller squares running from top left to bottom right, and the total number of spots in this line adds up to 18. The total number of spots in the diagonal line of six smaller squares running from top right to bottom left also adds up to 18. We've placed a few to give you a start, but can you place the rest?

[93] DIFFICULTY ✪✪✪✪✪✪✪✪✪✪  **3** Minutes

Can you answer these questions about the puzzle on page 77 without looking back?

1. How many girls are pictured?

2. How many girls have blond hair?

3. Which girls have pink bows in their hair?

4. How many girls with black hair are wearing white dresses?

5. How many girls with yellow bows are wearing a blue dress?

6. How many girls are wearing pink dresses?

7. Which girl is wearing a white dress and has white bows in her hair?

8. Which girls have the same color hair, dress, and bow?

95 DIFFICULTY ✪✪✪✪✪✪✪✪✪✪ **3** Minutes

One of these shopping baskets is different from the rest. Which is the odd one out?

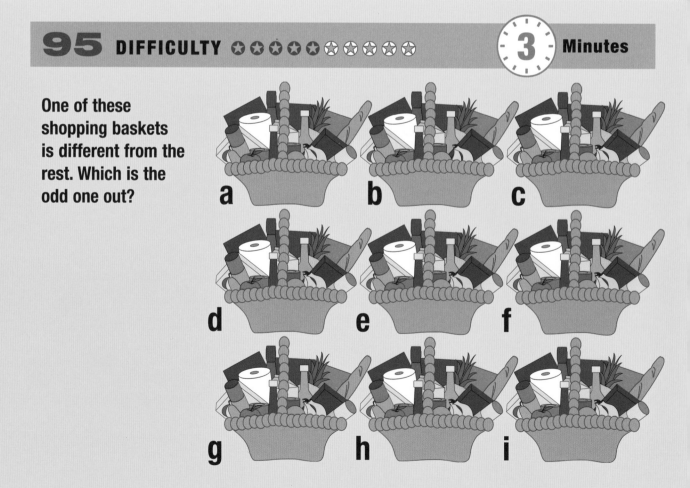

96 DIFFICULTY ✪✪✪✪✪✪✪☆☆☆ **5** Minutes

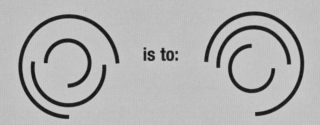

is to:

as

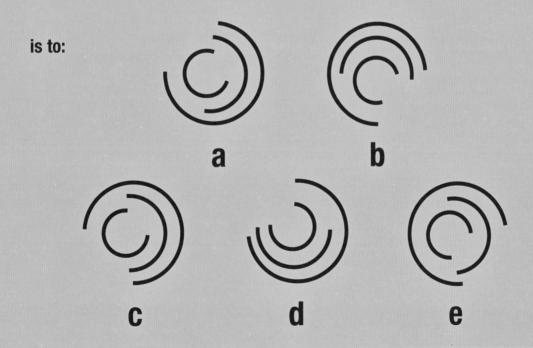

is to:

a

b

c

d

e

97 DIFFICULTY ✪✪✪✪✪✪✪✪☆☆  5 Minutes

Using the mortar lines, can you get from anywhere on the top of the wall to anywhere on the bottom?

98 **DIFFICULTY** ✪✪✪✪✪✪✩✩✩✩  **Minutes**

One of these stamps is different from the rest. Which is the odd one out?

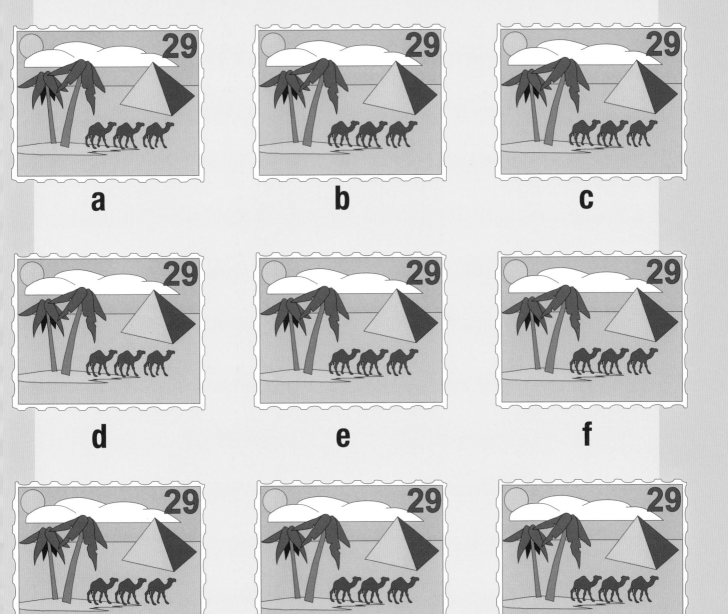

99 DIFFICULTY ✪✪✪✪✪✪✪✪✩✩    **3** Minutes

Jimmy's magic mirror reflects very strangely! Can you match each teapot to its correct (although misplaced and somewhat distorted) image in the mirror?

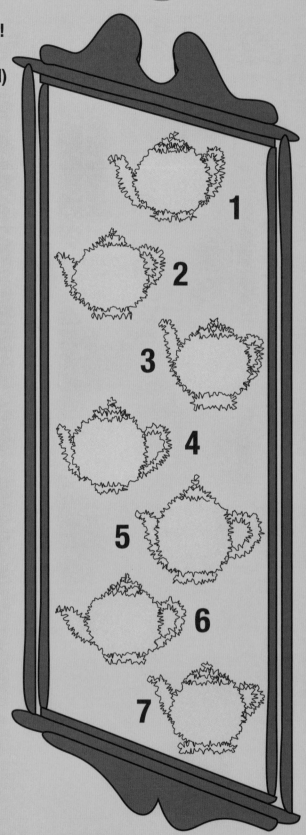

100 DIFFICULTY ✪✪✪✪✪✪✪✩✩  **5** Minutes

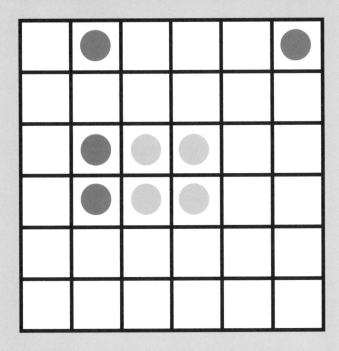

Can you divide this grid into four identical sections, each containing a red and a blue circle?

101 DIFFICULTY ✪✪✪✪✪✪✩✩✩ **7** Minutes

The square below contains exactly one of each of 36 faces from six standard dice. In each row, each column, and each main diagonal of smaller squares, there are faces with different numbers of spots. We've placed a few to give you a start, but can you place the rest?

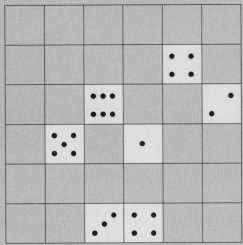

102 DIFFICULTY ✪✪✪✪✪✪✪✪✩✩  5 Minutes

Can you spot the nine differences between these two pictures? Circle them in the lower drawing.

103 DIFFICULTY ✪✪✪✪✪✪✪✪✪ ③ Minutes

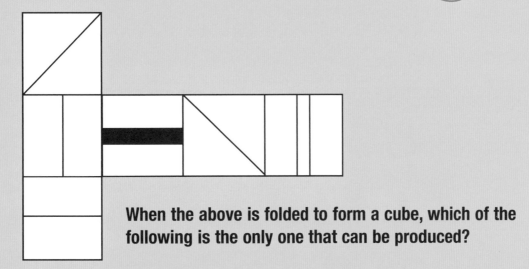

When the above is folded to form a cube, which of the following is the only one that can be produced?

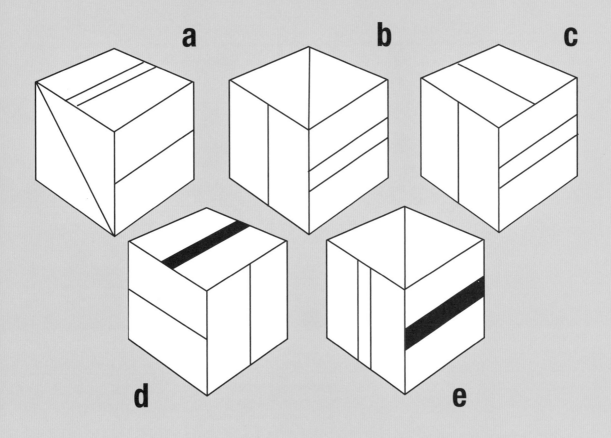

a

b

c

d

e

104 DIFFICULTY ✪✪✪✪✪✪✪✪✪

In this two-player network game, the players play on a grid of 5 x 6 or 6 x 5 dots as illustrated. Each player takes a turn to draw a short line between any two dots of his or her color. Play continues until neither player can make a valid move. Lines must not cross. The winner is the player who makes the longest network—in other words, the contiguous network with the largest number of lines between dots. In the example illustrated, the red player won by 29 lines to 13.

Example: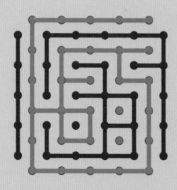

105 DIFFICULTY ✪✪✪✪✪✪✩✩✩  5 Minutes

Which of the four boxed figures (a, b, c, or d) completes the set?

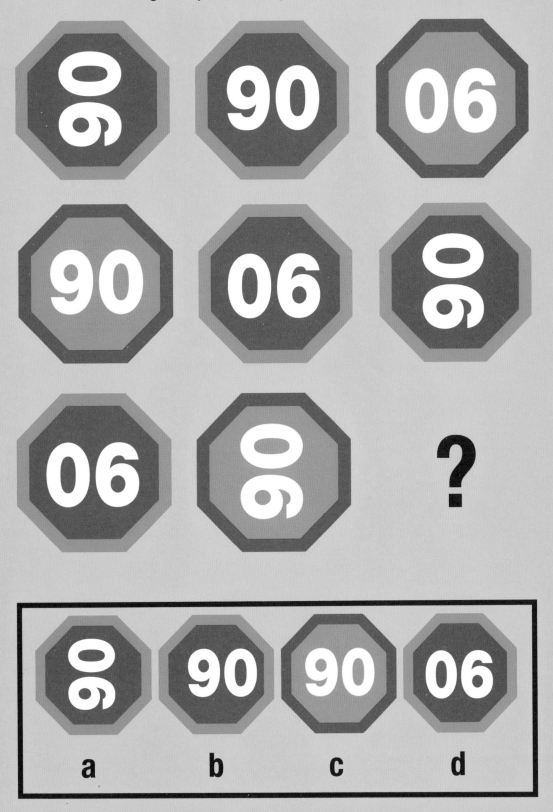

 **5** Minutes

Which two vases are identical?

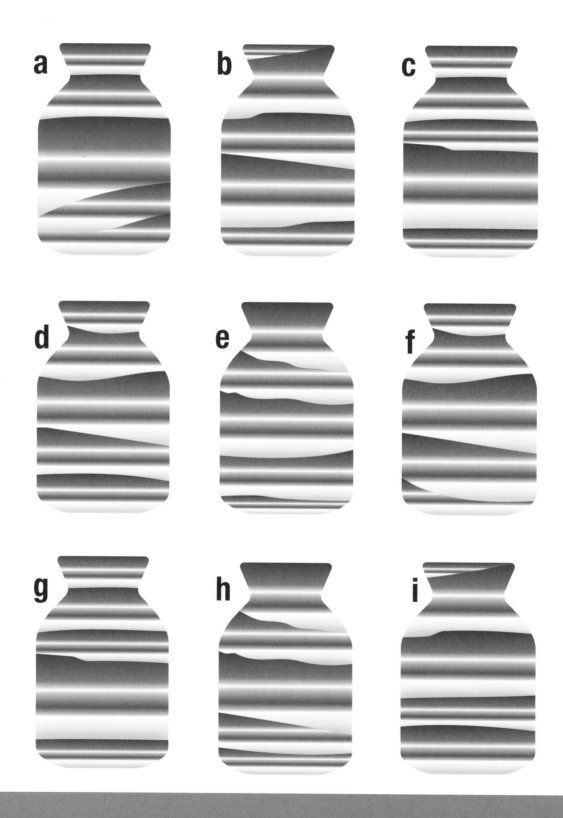

107 DIFFICULTY ✪✪✪✪✪✪✩✩✩ ⑤ Minutes

Jimmy's magic mirror reflects very strangely! Can you match each bottle of juice to its correct (although misplaced and somewhat distorted) image in the mirror?

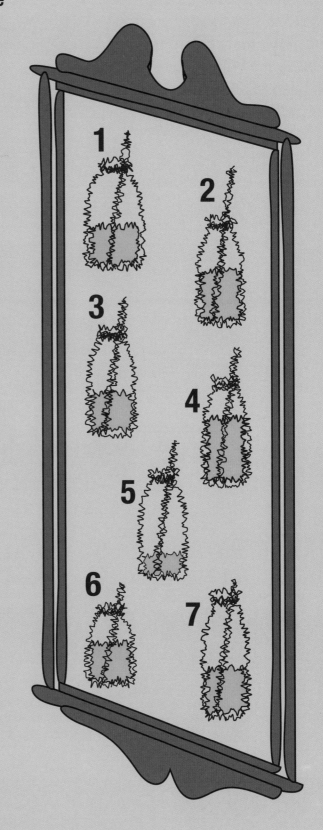

108 DIFFICULTY ✪✪✪✪✪✪✪✪✪✩   6 Minutes

Can you spot the eight differences between these two quilts? You may find this a little more difficult because the bottom quilt has been rotated. Mark the changes with an X in the lower quilt.

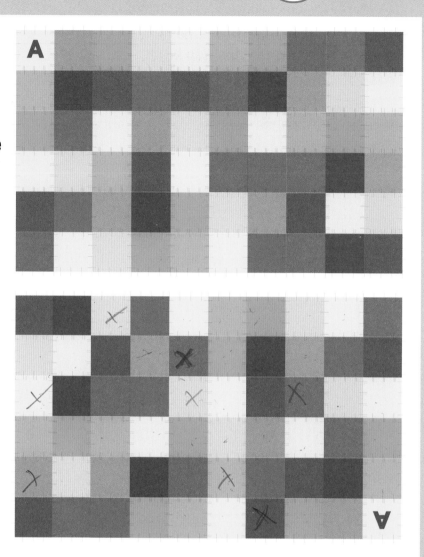

109 DIFFICULTY ✪✪✪✪✪✪✪✩✩✩   5 Minutes

Where can this specific ring of hexagons be found in the larger grid? The pattern may be rotated but not reflected.

110 DIFFICULTY ✪✪✪✪✪✪✫✫✫

The aim of this two-player game is to be the first to get four of your symbols in a line (horizontally, vertically, or diagonally). Unlike tic-tac-toe, both players choose a square at the same time by writing down their choice in secret. They then compare notes. If they chose different squares, they put their chosen player symbol in their chosen square. If the squares opted for happen to be the same, players have to vote again and must choose a different square.

There is one special rule: If a player has just one possibility of winning the game on the next move, he or she must go somewhere else and his opponent MUST choose that square instead. For example, in the game illustrated, it is obvious the Circle player would vote for d4 next to try to win the game. Therefore, the Star player must move to d4 and the Circle player must choose somewhere else. It is not necessary to write down the choices for this rule. This rule may seem unfair, but it saves time.

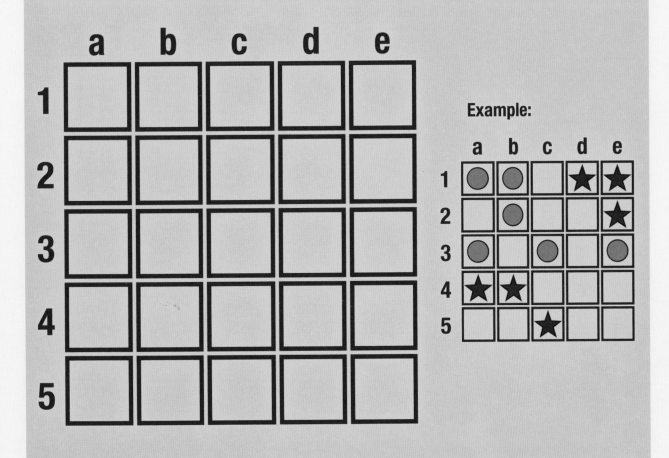

Example:

111 DIFFICULTY ✪✪✪✪✪✪✪✪☆☆  4 Minutes

Farmer Giles would like to buy two identical tractors. Can you help him? The two that are the same might even be reflections of one another, so look carefully!

a

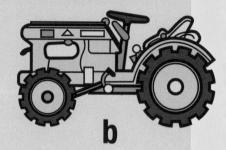

b

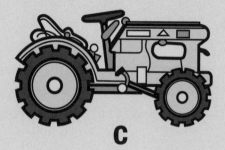

c

d

e

f

g

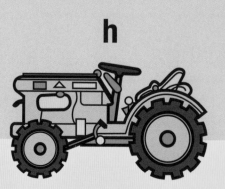

h

i

112 DIFFICULTY ✪✪✪✪✪✪☆☆☆☆  Minutes

Study this picture for two minutes, then see if you can answer the questions on page 94.

113 DIFFICULTY ✪✪✪✪✪✪☆☆☆☆  Minutes

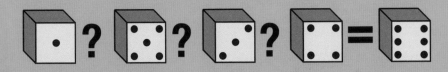

By placing three of the four different mathematical operators (+, -, x, ÷) between the dice in each of the following three calculations, can you arrive at the correct totals, as given?

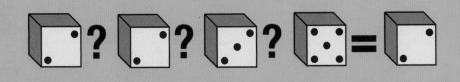

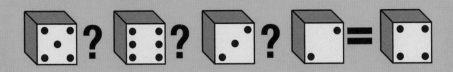

[112] DIFFICULTY ✪✪✪✪✪✪✪✪✪✪  3 Minutes

Can you answer these questions about the puzzle on page 93 without looking back?

1. Which shape is the most abundant?

2. How many circles have red borders and dark blue centers?

3. How many circles have red borders and green centers?

4. How many bordered shapes are there in total?

5. How many shapes have dark blue borders?

6. How many shapes have green borders?

7. How many squares have green borders?

8. What is the total number of red-bordered circles plus red-bordered stars?

114 DIFFICULTY ✪✪✪✪✪✪✪✪✪✪ 6 Minutes

All of these butterflies may look identical, but one is different from the rest. Which is the odd one out?

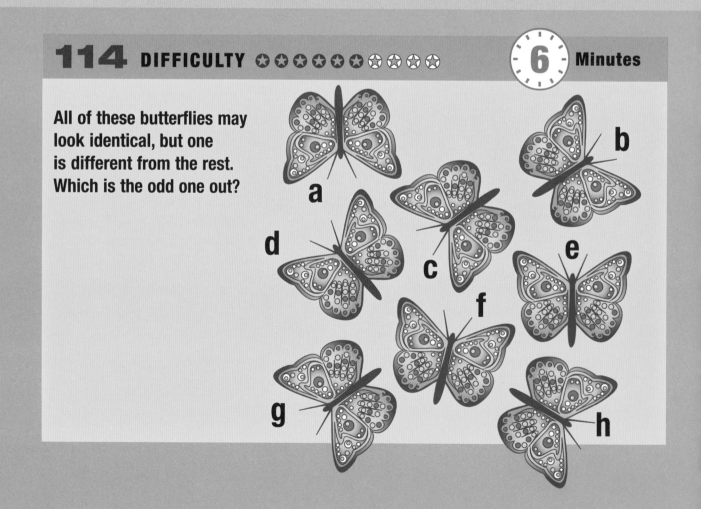

In each of the four buildings below, one type of brick is used more or less frequently than it is in the other three buildings. Can you determine the different brick in each construction? The ten brick types are as follows:

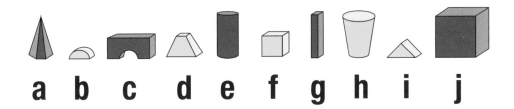

Building 1

Building 2

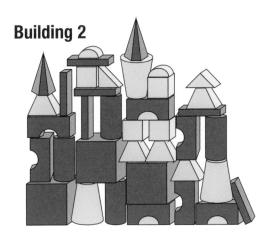

Building 3

Building 4

116 DIFFICULTY ✪✩✪✩✪✩✪✩✪✩✩  **5** Minutes

Which of the four boxed figures (a, b, c, or d) completes the set?

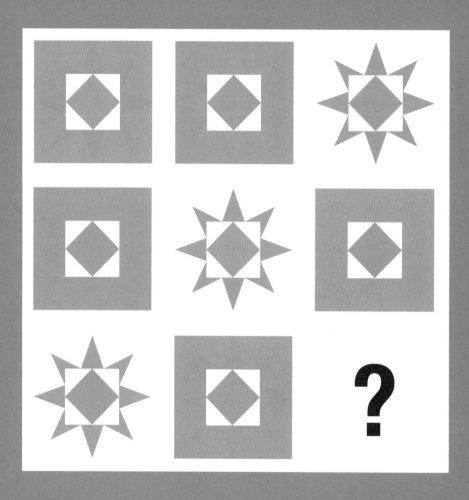

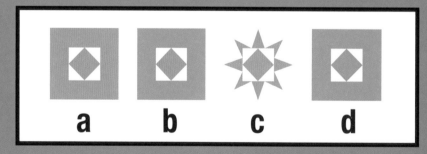

a   b   c   d

117 DIFFICULTY ✪✪✪✪✪✪✪✪☆☆  **Minutes**

Can you spot the eleven differences between these two pictures? Circle them in the drawing on the right.

118 DIFFICULTY ✪✪✪✪✪✪☆☆☆☆☆  **Minutes**

You have been presented with a tray bearing five bags that should each contain 100 gold coins, except you have been told that one of them contains only 99. You quickly arrange the bags to reveal the one that's short. How?

119 DIFFICULTY ✪✪✪✪✪✪✪✩✩ 6 Minutes

Which three sets of bricks will fit together to form a perfect cube of the same shape as this gray one?

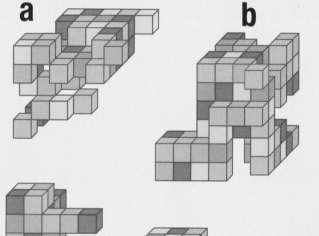

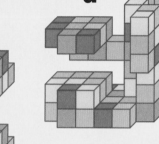

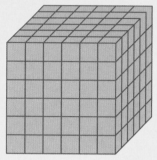

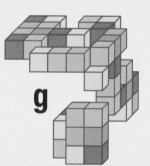

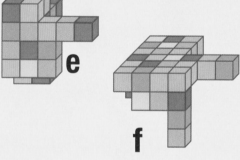

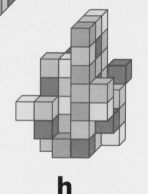

a

b

c

d

e

f

g

h

120 DIFFICULTY ✪✪✪✪✪✪✪✪✩ 6 Minutes

Can you divide this grid into five sections, each containing five different shapes of five different colors?

Which of the four boxed figures (a, b, c, or d) completes the set?

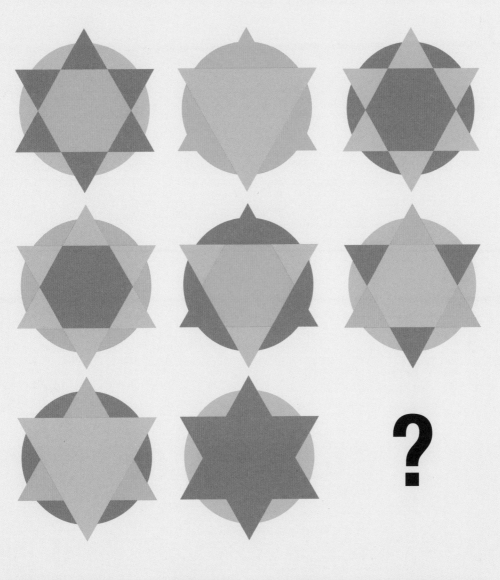

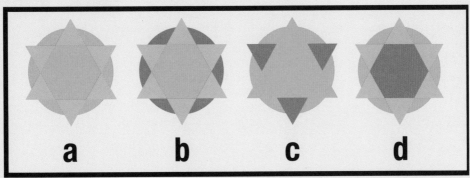

a   b   c   d

122 DIFFICULTY ✪✪✪✪✪✪✪☆☆☆  **8** Minutes

Find your way through this fortified maze to the chair in the central chamber.

123 DIFFICULTY ✪✪✪✪✪✪✪✩✩✩ ⏱ 5 Minutes

At first glance, these patios may look identical, although they have been photographed from different angles. However, only two are identical. Can you spot them?

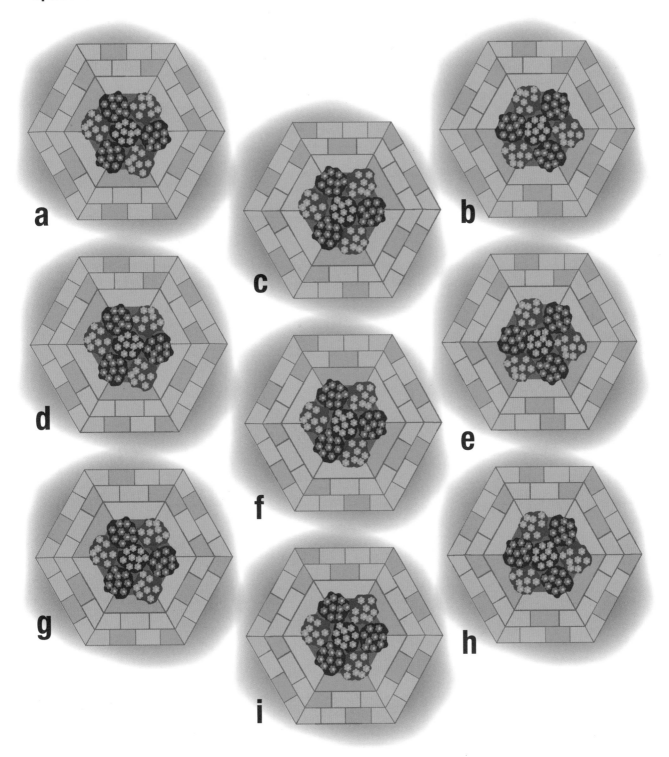

124 DIFFICULTY ✩✩✩✩✩✩✩✩✩✩ ③

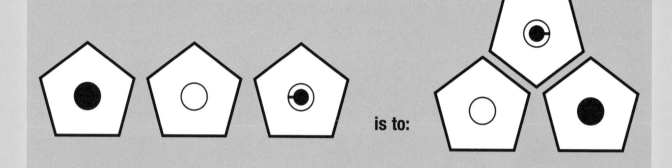

is to:

as

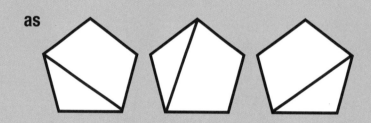

is to:

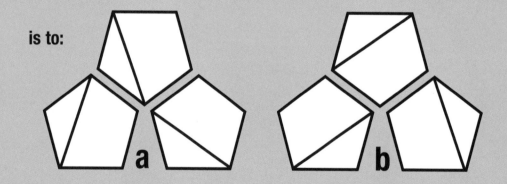

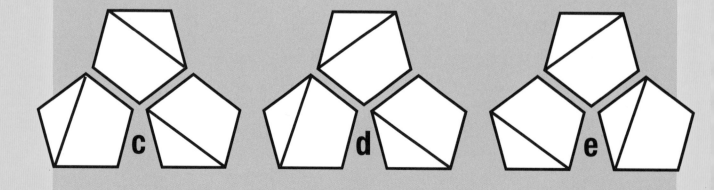

125 DIFFICULTY ✪✩✪✩✪✩✪✩✪✩

To play this wall-building game, you need to draw a set of approximately 25 connected regions. We've done this by drawing overlapping circles, but it really doesn't matter what your "map" looks like.

Two players take turns drawing a wall that connects three unused regions. The first player that cannot make a valid move loses the game.

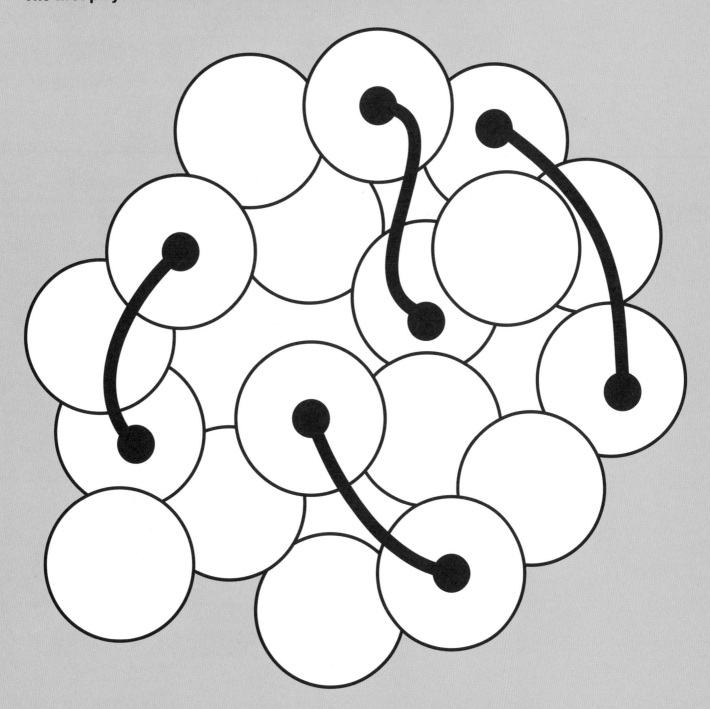

126 DIFFICULTY ✩✩✩✩✩✩✩✩✩✩ ⏱ 6 Minutes

Without rotating or reflecting any, can you spot which three hexagons are identical in color?

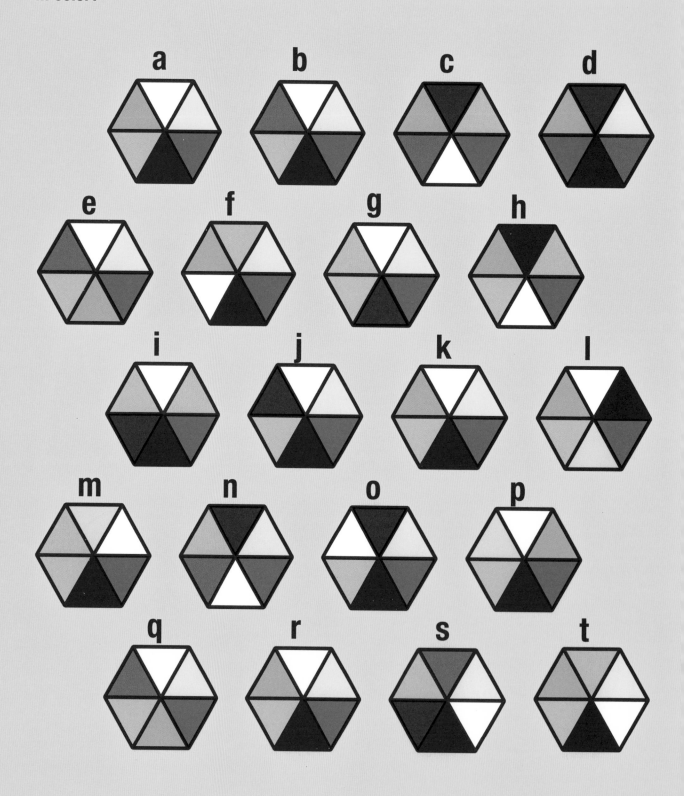

127 DIFFICULTY ✪✪✪✪✪✪✪✩✩✩  5 Minutes

Which of the four boxed figures (a, b, c, or d) completes the set?

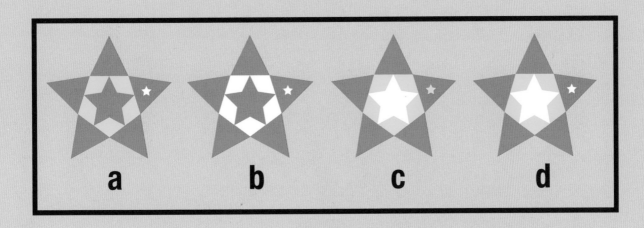

a   b   c   d

ANSWERS

1

2

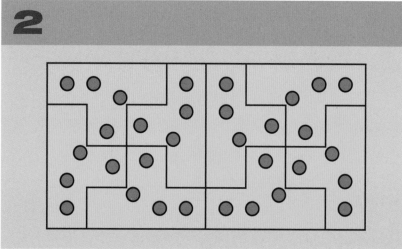

3

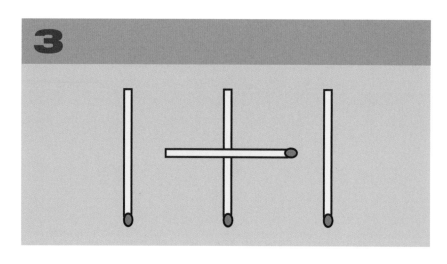

4

 **a**

5

 c; each vertical and horizontal line contains one shape with all green triangles, one with all pink triangles, and one with half pink and half green triangles. Each line also contains two shapes with a red dot in the center and one with no red dot. The missing shape must have all green triangles and a red dot.

6

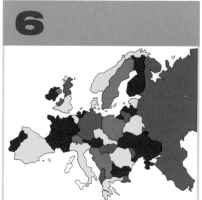

7

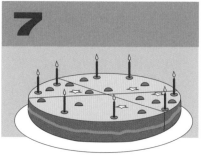

8

Kirsty wins in the fewest moves.

9

a=5, b=7, c=1, d=3, e=2, f=6, and g=4

10

Place stepping stones on the grid rather than making consecutive steps.

11

Building 1
e

Building 2
g

Building 3
h

Building 4
b

12

Gary won $8. The total payback is the number of spots on the opposite side of the first die multiplied by the number of spots on the opposite side of the second. Thus Gary got back $20 (5 x 4 = 20), winning $8.

13

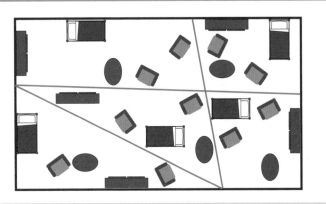

14

 If you color in the areas like a political map, you will see that x and y are different colored areas. This means that since x is inside the loop, y is outside the loop.

15

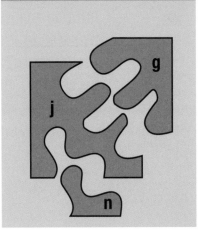

16

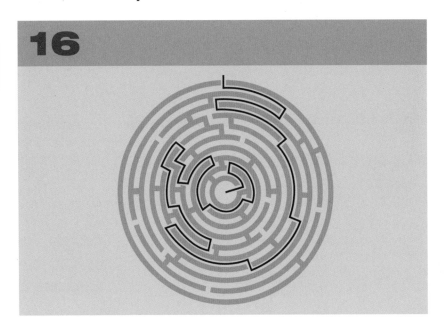

17

18

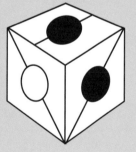

d; all figures originally outside the hexagon transfer to the inside of the hexagon, and vice versa. Also, black circles turn to white triangles, white circles turn to black triangles, and vice versa.

19

C

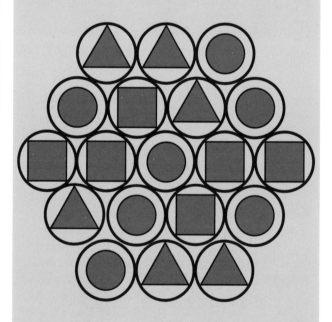

20

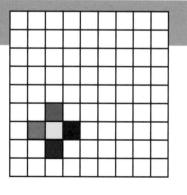

21

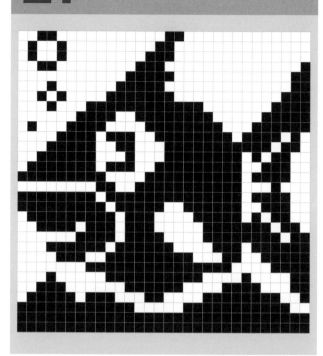

22

A circle. Every triangle of six circles, or , must contain different numbers of circles, squares, and triangles.

23

There are ten differences between the two pictures.

24

([6 + 4] ÷ 5) − 1 = 1
([2 + 6] - 5) x 1 = 3
([4 x 4] ÷ 2) − 3 = 5

25

e

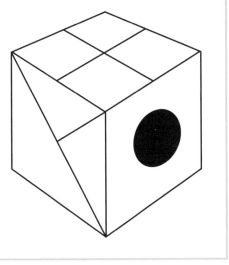

26

1. Blue
2. 3
3. Green
4. 3

5. 2
6. 8
7. 2
8. 25

27

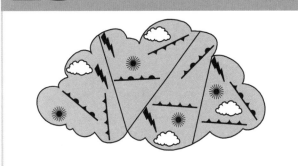

28

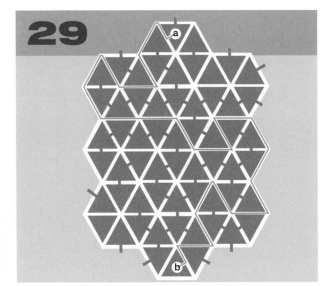

29

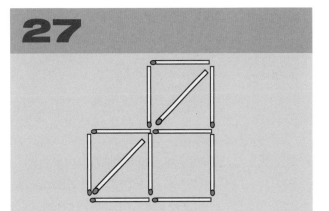

30

A circle. Each row and column, across and down, has thirteen corners.

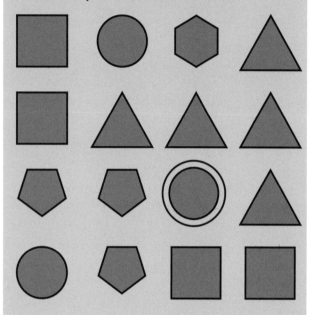

31

a; the circles on the line at the extreme left change places. The line on the extreme right points down instead of up.

32

a; it is looking in a different direction.

33

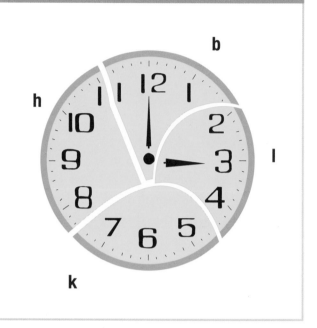

34

1. 36	5. 3
2. c and f	6. d
3. 11	7. 5
4. b	8. b

35

36

None. Rearrange them as follows:

37

48; multiply the number of dots on the top face of each die by the total of the number of dots on the (visible) front and side, then deduct the sum of the dots on the three hidden faces of each die.

38

22; Angelica can see the top faces of all three dice, thus a total of nine spots. The opposite sides of a die have spots that add up to seven. On the left die, the side face Angelica can see has six spots. On the central die, the side face Angelica can see has two spots. On the right die, the side face Angelica can see also has two spots. On the bottom face of the right die there is one spot, so the end face of this die (hidden from you) has either three or four spots. If this end face has four spots, then the total number of spots Angelica can see is twenty-three. But Angelica can see a different number of spots than you—and you can see twenty-three. So the end face Angelica can see has three spots. Thus,

Angelica can see a total of nine spots on the top faces, ten spots on the side faces, and three on the end face for a combined total of twenty-two spots.

39

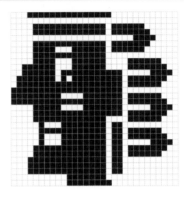

40

a=6, b=7, c=4, d=5, e=2, f=1, and g=3

41

d

42

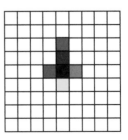

43

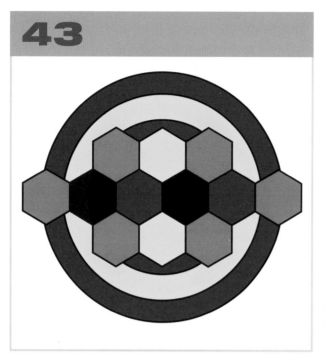

46

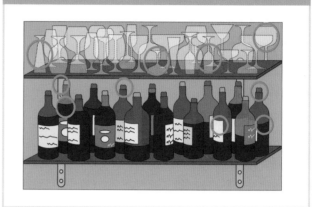

47

c and i

44

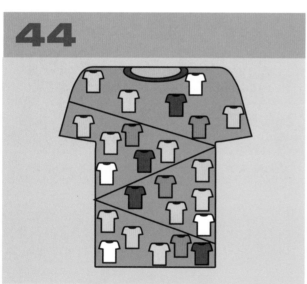

48

Building 1
a

Building 2
c

Building 3
i

Building 4

  b

45

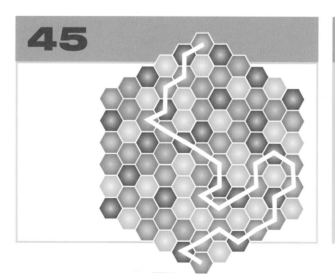

49

  a; where shapes touch the side of the square, the shape in the adjacent square must also touch.

50

1. M
2. Yellow
3. Red
4. Red
5. B
6. L
7. Black
8. 0

51

Put them on their edges.

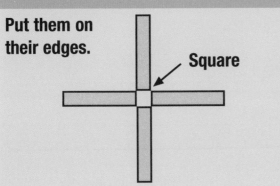

Square

52

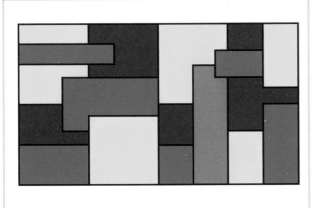

53

Drawing lines inside existing loops will reduce the length of the game but won't guarantee you a win. It's best to plan carefully.

54

b; the image is the same except that each white arm that points down in the original now points up, and vice versa.

55

56

d

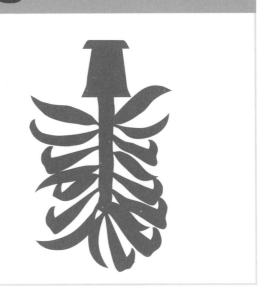

57

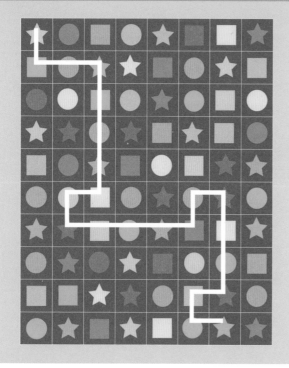

58

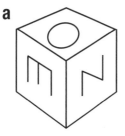

59

a

60

f; the points of the central three stars are not aligned.

61

62

f; the figure in the middle rotates 180° and turns from black to white. The three small white squares become one large black square and enclose the figure in the middle.

63

Gary won $4. The total payback is double the difference of the number of spots on the two dice. Thus Gary got back $10: (6 − 1) x 2 = 10, winning $4.

64

1. 5
2. Blue
3. Green
4. White
5. S

6. 3: the T, the S, and the W
7. 2
8. T

65

1=d, 2=f, 3=b, 4=a, 5=c, 6=e

66

There are 21 dots on each die, thus a total of 84 dots on the four dice. Since 34 dots are visible, the total number of dots on the sides that are not visible amounts to 50.

67

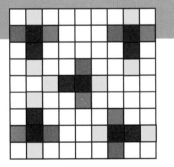

68

Tom wins in the fewest moves.

69

70

g; the bottom two stripes on her shirt are different.

71

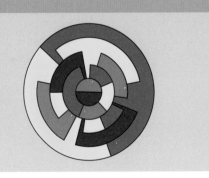

72

The minute hand of the clock in the bottom-right corner is incorrect. It should be pointing at the five minutes to the hour position. Now each hour hand points to the minute hand on one of the other clocks so that they lie on the same extended line.

73

a and c

74

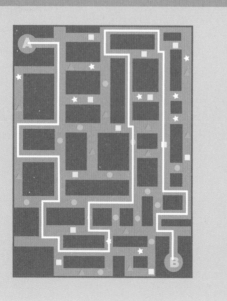

75

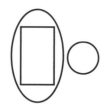

d; the figure in the middle (the rectangle) reduces in size, rotates 90°, and goes inside the figure originally at the bottom (the oval), which increases in size. The figure at the top (the circle) attaches itself to the right-hand side of the oval.

76

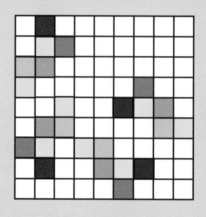

77

78

c and f

79

80

The triangle can be seen to consist of four isosceles triangles, each side being one match in length. The hexagon consists of six of the same-sized triangles, which is twice as big in area.

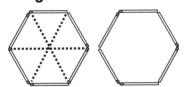

81

c; on each row and column, each shape and each color appears three times.

82

c, h, and k

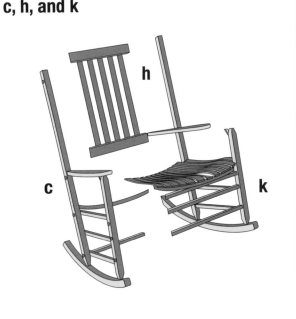

83

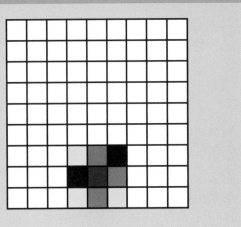

84

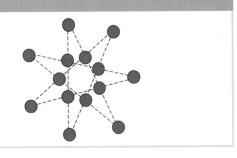

85

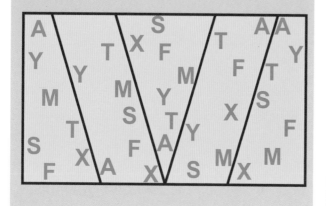

86

i

87

1. 2
2. 7
3. 3
4. Yellow
5. 2
6. 5
7. 25
8. 8

88

4; add the number of spots on the three visible faces of each die, then do the same for the hidden faces of each die. Now deduct the lower total from the higher total and multiply that answer by four.

89

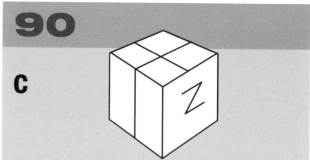

90

C

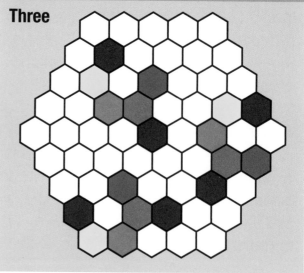

91

Three

92

f

93

1. 9
2. 4
3. d, f, and h
4. 2
5. 1
6. 2
7. c
8. a and i

94

In the diagonal top left to bottom right, there is no 5, so in column 1, the 5 is in row 3, and in row 2, the 5 is in column 3. Thus in row 1, 5 is in column 5, and in column 2, the 5 is in row 5. By elimination, in row 2, the 6 is in column 4, so 6 is also in row 3/column 5, column 1/row 4, and column 3/row 5. Column 5 has 2 in row 4 and 3 in row 6. The number of spots

2	6	4	3	5	1
1	3	5	6	4	2
5	4	2	1	6	3
6	1	3	4	2	5
3	5	6	2	1	4
4	2	1	5	3	6

in row 4/column 4 is (by elimination) either 1 or 4 and for a total of 18 spots, if 1 is in row 4/column 4, there would need to be either 6 + 2 or 4 + 4 in the top two squares of that diagonal line. There is a 6 in row 1/column 2, so neither of the top two squares in the diagonal can contain a 6, and since there is 4 in row 2/column 5, there can't be 4 in row 2/column 2. Thus (above) in the diagonal running top left to bottom right, there isn't a 1 in row 4/column 4. Thus row 4/column 4 has 4 and (for a total of 18), the top two squares in that diagonal have 2 and/or 3. The 3 isn't in column 1 (there is already a 3 in that column), so column 1/row 1 is 2 and column 2/row 2 is

3. By elimination, column 1/row 6 is 4, so row 6/column 3 is 1, and row 6/column 2 is 2. Thus (by elimination), column 2/row 4 is 1, column 2/row 3 is 4, row 1/column 3 is 4, row 5/column 4 is 2, row 5/column 6 is 4, and row 2/column 6 is 2. In the diagonal top right to bottom left, spots total 18, so row 1/column 6 is 1 and row 3/column 4 is 1. Thus row 1/column 4 is 3 and row 3/column 6 is 3.

95

b

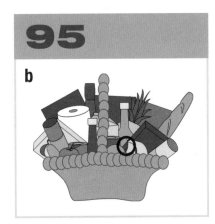

96

e; the large arc rotates 90° clockwise, and the other two arcs rotate 180°.

97

98

h

99

a = 2   e = 7
b = 4   f = 5
c = 6   g = 3
d = 1

100

101

In the diagonal top right to bottom left there is a 4, so in column 3/row 4 there is (by elimination) a 2. In the diagonal top left to bottom right, 4 is in row 1, and column 6/row 6 contains 5. In row 4, 4 is in column 6. In the diagonal top right to bottom left, 5 is in row 3, and column 2/row 5 contains 4. There are six 4s, so the remaining 4 is in column 3/row 5. In row 5, 5 is in column 1; so in row 2, 5 is in column 3, thus 5 is in column 5/row 1, thus row 1 has 1 in column 3. Since there is now 2 in the diagonal top right to bottom left, there isn't 2 in column 1/row 6; so in column 1, 2 is in row 2. Thus in the diagonal top left to bottom right, 3 is in column 2/row 2, and 2 is in column 5/row 5. Remaining 2s are in column 4/row 1 and column 2/row 6. By elimination, row 1 has 6 in column 2 and 3 in column 6. In the top

right/bottom left diagonal, 6 is in row 6, so 1 is in row 5. In column 1, 1 is in row 3 and 3 is in row 4. In row 3, 3 is in column 5. In column 5, 6 is in row 4 and 1 is in row 6. In column 6, 6 is in row 5 and 1 is in row 2, so row 2 has 6 in column 4 and column 4 has 3 in row 5.

102

103

d

104

Don't spread yourself too thinly.
One good network will beat several
smaller ones.

105

b: each vertical and horizontal
line contains one shape the
right way up, one rotated
through 90°, and one rotated through
180°. Each line also contains one red
shape with a blue outline and two blue
shapes with a red outline. The missing
shape should be the right way up and
blue with a red outline.

90

106

c and g

107

a = 4   e = 7
b = 3   f = 6
c = 5   g = 2
d = 1

108

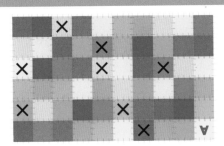

109

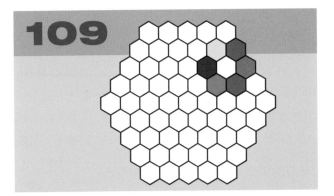

110

An easy way to win is to create a line of
three in the middle of the grid. Your
opponent can't cover both ends at once.

111

c and d

112

1. The star   5. 2
2. 1   6. 3
3. 2   7. None
4. 14   8. 4

113

(1 x 5) − 3 + 4 = 6
(2 x 2) + 3 − 5 = 2
(5 + 6 − 3) ÷ 2 = 4

114

e

115

Building 1	Building 2	Building 3	Building 4

b   a   i   f

116

b: each vertical and horizontal line contains one blue, one turquoise, and one white outer box. Each line also contains one blue inner diamond and two turquoise ones. Finally, each line contains one blue star and two turquoise ones. The missing image should be a green outer box with a purple inner diamond and a green star.

117

118

Balance the tray on one bag, then place the other four bags as shown. The bag on the part of the tray that rises is light. If it stays level, then the bag underneath is the light one, which contains 99 coins.

119

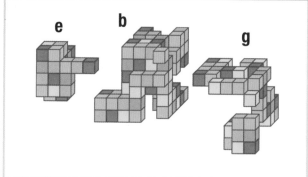

e   b   g

120

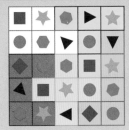

121

a; each vertical and horizontal line contains one light green, one dark green, and one orange circle. Each line also contains one light green, one dark green, and one orange hexagon. Each line contains right-side-up triangles in light green, dark green, and orange. Finally, each line contains two inverted triangles in light green and one in dark green. The missing image should be of an orange circle with an orange hexagon and both triangles in light green.

122

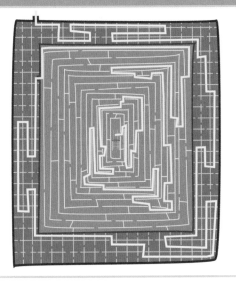

123

c and h

124

d; the pentagon on the left goes to the bottom right, the pentagon on the right goes to the top, having rotated 180°, and the pentagon in the middle goes to the bottom left.

125

The first few moves don't matter. The skill lies in planning your end game.

126

a, k, and r

127

c; each vertical and horizontal line contains one white pentagon and two yellow ones, one white inner star and two red ones, and one small yellow star and two small white ones. The missing shape should have a yellow pentagon, a white inner star, and a small yellow star.

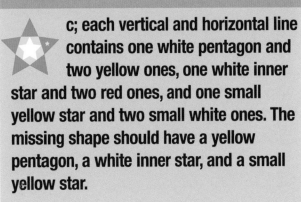

ACKNOWLEDGMENTS ✪ PERPLEXING PERCEPTIONS

✪ Puzzle contributors

Contributors are listed next to the numbers of the puzzles they created.

✪ Brainwarp

Puzzles 3, 22, 27, 30, 36, 49, 51, 58, 80, 81, 84, 118

✪ David Bodycombe

Puzzles 6, 10, 14, 20, 42, 43, 52, 53, 67, 71, 72, 76, 83, 89, 90, 104, 109, 110, 125

✪ Guy Campbell

Puzzles 1, 5, 16, 21, 29, 39, 45, 55, 57, 74, 77, 97, 105, 121, 122, 127

✪ Philip Carter

Puzzles 18, 19, 25, 31, 54, 59, 62, 75, 91, 96, 103, 124

✪ Puzzler Media Ltd

Puzzles 2, 4, 7, 8, 9, 11, 12, 13, 15, 17, 23, 24, 26, 28, 32, 33, 34, 35, 37, 38, 40, 41, 44, 46, 47, 48, 50, 56, 60, 61, 63, 64, 65, 66, 68, 69, 70, 73, 78, 79, 82, 85, 86, 87, 88, 92, 93, 94, 95, 98, 99, 100, 101, 102, 106, 107, 108, 111, 112, 113, 114, 115, 116, 117, 119, 120, 123, 126

Perplexing Perceptions was commissioned, edited, designed, and produced by:
Book Creation Ltd., 20 Lochaline Street, London W6 9SH, United Kingdom
Managing Director: Hal Robinson
Editor: David Popey **Art Editor:** Keith Miller
Designer: Justin Hunt **Copy Editor:** Sarah Barlow **Editorial Assistant:** Claire Bratt